Doing the Right Thing
Without Permission

50 Methods to Achieve Success

Bill and Cindy Perry

EABooks Publishing
Your Partner In Publishing

WARNING: This book may require you to step out of your comfort zone.

Doing theRight Thing Without Permission
50 Methods to Achieve Success
Copyright © 2025 Bill & Cindy Perry
All rights reserved.

ISBN: 978-1-966382-18-8
LCCN: 2025908405

Cover design: Robin Black
Cover illustration: bo feng

Published by EABooks Publishing, a division of
Living Parables of Central Florida, Inc. a 501c3
EABooksPublishing.com

To Bob Ousnamer

Bob Ousnamer, a senior staff member at EABooks, picked up a copy of our book, *How to Manage Management*, read it, and said, "This is a great book, and still is needed— even more than in the1970s."

He strongly told us to update the book, and said he would like for EABooks to publish it. It took two years, but the book is much better today, emphasizing doing the right thing. Thank you, Bob!

Contents

How to Make Things Happen When You Don't Have the Authority

THERE ARE TWO WAYS to lead.

One is having the authority to make someone do something they don't want to do. This is necessary in the military, but not always effective in the business world.

The other way is leading by influencing others. *Influence* is the ability to shape outcomes and behaviors, usually by subtle means unknown to the person being influenced.

To see how such influence plays out in practice, let's examine a case study.

Dr. Ben Carson is a neurosurgeon and former US secretary of Housing and Urban Development. Early in his career, as a resident in a hospital, he was faced with an urgent situation.

A young boy was brought into the emergency room for treatment. He had been hit in the head several times with a baseball bat, and incurred extensive swelling of the brain. Dr. Carson was acting head of the ER that shift, because a major doctors' conference was in session. He knew what operation needed to be performed, but as a resident he was not authorized to operate, and had never performed that particular operation.

Unable to reach any doctor, he had a dilemma. Operate, and risk losing his medical career, or put the boy in the intensive care unit until a doctor was available and hope for the best.

After praying about the situation, he decided to operate. His operation saved the boy's brain.

When asked why he took the risk, he answered, "Because it was the right thing to do."

Was he punished? No. In fact, he was called a hero.

Some people can only lead after they are given authority. By using Manage Management Tactics, you can lead by influencing others—by recognizing things you have done to succeed without having permission. If you want examples of people who had a major influence on others, see what has been done by Dr. Martin Luther King, or Mohandas Gandhi, or Jesus, each of whom influenced millions of people without having any authority to do so.

Strategies and Tactics

Work is an activity, physical or mental, that is done to create a result. That result may be a product or a process, but ideally, the result of work ads benefit to the world. A *worker* is one doing the work, whether a profession, trade, or craft.

For example, my wife is a craftswoman who puts together three-hundred-piece picture puzzles. Industrial engineers would define the place she performs her work as a *workstation*. My wife's workstation is a kitchen table. Before she begins work, she has a requirement, which is putting together a picture puzzle from a box filled with pieces. She only begins work when she knows the requirement, which is to put all the pieces together until the result matches the picture on the top of the puzzle box.

She has developed a *strategy* to put the puzzle together. A strategy is an approach to managing or planning. When my wife works on assembling a puzzle, she uses two *tactics*: First, put the border of the puzzle together, and second, sort large segments of the puzzle by color before putting them together. The puzzle box does not tell her to do that—she has developed her own plan (strategy) and practices (tactics) for putting picture puzzles together, and she is very good at it.

How to Manage Management is a strategy—an approach—to accomplishing your goals in the workplace. Tactics are the individual techniques and practices one uses to fulfill the strategy. In this book we call each technique a **Manage Management Tactic** or **MMT**. I wrote this book to provide you with effective tools to use in business when you want to do the right thing. These practices are designed to help workers when rules and roadblocks stop them from doing what needs to be done.

CHAPTER ONE

Manage Management Tactics are Miracle Makers

Using the How to Manage Management strategy
makes the impossible possible.

I SPENT FIVE YEARS at Kodak learning how to control and audit computer systems. In 1973, when I filled a new position at the Institute of Internal Auditors, my first assignment was to get a $50,000 grant to fund a project about controlling and auditing computer systems. Up to that point, the most the IIA had ever spent on a research project was $1,000. IBM was Kodak's supplier for computers, so I went to them to get my grant.

My IBM contact knew immediately that this project was needed, but told me to ask for $500,000 rather than $50,000, because then it would require top IBM management support—only at that level would they realize the ways the project could benefit IBM.

I got the $500,000, and was told by my boss that I had "pulled off a miracle."

Do miracles still happen today? Yes!

A miracle is any occurrence that apparently contradicts known scientific laws, hence they are often attributed to supernatural causes.

If you are working with a faulty computer system and need help, but no one is available, then that afternoon your boss calls you to tell you the company's top technician just finished his job early and is available to help you—that's a miracle.

Most people just want things to improve—they are not looking for a miracle, they just want a better life. People seeking improvement are not looking for a contradiction of scientific laws. They are seeking something that's not currently being used, but that when it is used produces a result that makes what looked impossible, possible.

Thomas A. Edison learned a hundred ways not to make a light-bulb, and once he succeeded, light bulbs showered light on the 1899 World's Fair in Chicago. Edison said he just kept trying until finally found a light bulb that worked. Was that a miracle, or just hard work? To those who had never seen a light bulb before, it was a miracle.

Doug Flute, a college football quarterback, needed to score a touchdown in the last few seconds to win the game. He threw a pass more than forty yards into the end zone, hoping one of his teammates would be there to catch the ball. One did. That pass has been called a "Hail Mary Pass" ever since.

To those watching these events, what was done seemed impossible, yet somehow what these athletes did worked. Both Edison and Flute were confident in what they were doing. They were confident because they knew things their competition did not know and they trusted the skills of their colleagues.

Three thousand years ago a small farm boy named David volunteered to fight the giant Goliath. King Saul advised David to wear armor, but he refused. The armor was clunky and ill-fitting. David knew he needed to be nimble, so he faced Goliath without it. He nevertheless killed Goliath with nothing but a slingshot. He later went on to be king.

Miracle Case Studies

We can be confident that Manage Management Tactics (MMTs) work because they have been used successfully before. Let's look at the type of Manage Management Tactics that are used every day without most people being aware that the practice might be new to their employer.

In the 1960s, Captain Grace Hopper of the US Navy felt she should take action on problems, but for many reasons could not get permission from her superiors to take them. The military is very strict on the chain of command. Knowing this, Captain Hopper believed that doing what was right would not be punished. She developed a principle called, "It is easier to get forgiveness than permission." She used this tactic regularly, without any repercussions.

My team once worked overtime without extra pay for many weeks to complete a very difficult computer project on time and within budget. I asked my boss if he would approve $2,000 for a celebration party for my team and their spouses, knowing my boss would cut my request in half, because that's what he did most of the time. I only needed $1,000, so I used the Double Cut Theory—asking for twice what I wanted, expecting only to get half of my request. I got the $1,000. Every one of my team members were thrilled to be recognized for what they had accomplished.

My best friend at work was totally frustrated by his micromanager boss. I told him to use The Information Avalanche Tactic. This practice entails sending your boss emails twice every day explaining what you are doing and why. My friend never heard from his micromanager boss after that.

CHAPTER TWO

Why Risk It?

Who in Their Right Mind Would Manage Management?

IF MMTS ARE PRACTICED somewhere every day with positive results, why aren't they taught in business colleges and MBA programs? Business schools have curriculums based on good business practices. There is no room in their curriculums for teaching the practices needed to circumvent bad management.

Bad mangers often follow mistaken practices, such as micromanaging subordinates or failing to prevent poor employees from shortcutting work while good workers are inhibited from finishing on time and within budget. Poor management practices put good workers in the position of either following what their boss wants them to do until their project is in crisis, or taking initiative to use an MMT to get things done in a manner that is in the best interest of all concerned.

Why would anyone take the risk of using an MMT?

Sometimes you cannot get a manager to approve what you believe, given the circumstances, is the right thing to do. There are many reasons this might be the case:

- The manager you need to get approval from is not available.
- The approval paperwork will take too long to meet requirements.
- Your boss is not willing to take risks on new business practices.
- The product or technique you want to employ was not developed by your company and is therefore not pre-approved.
- What you want to do was tried before and didn't work, therefore it is perceived as "no good."
- Your boss will let you try it—if it works they will take the credit, and if it doesn't it's your fault.
- What you want to do is improve your personal capabilities, which will have no impact on your job but will make you more marketable in the future.

This book contains fifty MMTs, all of which are in use and, in my opinion, effective, proven business practices. That said, if they were better known their effectiveness might be diminished. I learned these tactics over the course of my seventy years working in a variety of venues—the military, public accounting, large and small corporations, nonprofit organizations, and in my own business for thirty years. I can no longer document where each one came from. In some cases, the person who taught them to me does not want to be known. Some I read in business journals or heard at conferences. Some I just don't remember where I got them. Some I invented myself.

Manage Management Tactics enable employees to successfully maneuver around weaknesses in entrenched business practices. Use these proven techniques to innovate new ways of work, perhaps without permission, to achieve your goals.

Doing the Right Thing

In ancient Britain, armored knights on horseback were the most feared fighting force in the world. Their motto was "might makes right," meaning the strongest forces could determine right from wrong. When King Arthur formed the Round Table, their motto became "might for right," meaning they would only fight for the right causes.

Good workers often face challenges when trying to do what is right for their organization. Too many bosses in today's world still believe they have the might to make their subordinates do whatever they want, regardless of whether it's right.

For example, one day my wife's boss told her to lie about his location if his wife called while he and his secretary were out "playing." He thought he had enough might to force her to lie. He was wrong. She quit.

Most organizations do not trust their employees, so they build systems to track employee behavior. Employees are often required to check in with what time they arrived for work, when they take breaks, and what time they leave work. The message employees get is that hours spent in the workplace are more important than what work is accomplished.

These regulations also inhibit creativity. If you and your colleagues are having a meaningful discussion about work during your thirty-minute lunch period, you still have to stop and get "back to work" on time.

Dr. W. Edwards Deming, a major pioneer in quality assurance, stated that if you do not trust a worker, fire them, but do not punish your good workers with regulations that inhibit them from doing their jobs. Dr. Deming also stated that performance appraisals are one of the most destructive business practices.

In many organizations, each employee has three jobs: the job they were hired to do, the job they must do to get their tasks done, and the job they are evaluated on. For example, my personal assistant did not like to gossip, so she avoided getting drawn into such conversations with her coworkers—how was I to evaluate her on the performance criteria "gets along well with coworkers?"

I had a boss who wanted, but did not require, his staff to come in every Saturday morning to show they were so dedicated to the organization they would put in extra time. I didn't go in on Saturdays. If you wonder how I was evaluated by my boss, don't. It wasn't good. I left the company because of how I was treated despite doing exceptional work.

A good friend of mine, Rebecca, was a teacher and narrowly escaped a run-in with an armed student. She quit teaching. Her message to me was that the worst thing an organization can do you is fire you. If you can accept that risk, then do what you know is the right thing.

I took that message to heart and started doing what I knew was in the best interest of my organization . . . and got fired from two different organizations after being recognized for exceptional work. However, my boss in each organizations thought they should get the credit for my work.

All I am telling you is that you may have to leave your comfort zone to deploy an MMT, even if it's for the right cause. Small MMTs only require a little risk, while major ones can be a great risk to you. Just use common sense and focus on doing the right thing.

Who Would Risk It?

So who would risk managing management? Those who are prepared. Preparation time can vary, but this book is designed to get you started.

As a young boy I had my own business, so when I worked for corporations after graduating from college, I was never really happy for working for bosses I thought were incompetent. For over twenty years, God kept moving me around, sometimes to jobs I did not want to do—but did them.

I had to deploy many MMTs to keep advancing, because my bosses were hindering me from doing an efficient and effective job. After twenty years of preparation for doing what God wanted me to do (although at the time, I did not realize that) I was ready to start my own business. It was very successful.

Some MMTs were easy to follow—for example Captain Hopper's, "It is easier to get forgiveness than permission." I used that within a few days. Others, for example "The Rathole Theory" (Chapter Eight), required more knowledge: in this case you need a basic understanding of accounting.

In my opinion, there are three prerequisites for successfully employing an MMT. First, you must be able to do your current job well, because if you cannot do that, the probability of using an MMT successfully is greatly diminished. Second, you must have confidence in your abilities to try new ways to succeed. Third, you must be using the MMT in the best interests of the company and those it serves, not your own interests, although in the end MMTs usually benefit you also if they are successful. Let's look at these three prerequisites individually:

Can you do your current job well? This is important because it defines how your organization evaluates you. If you have an eight-year-old daughter who is diligent about doing her homework, you know you can trust her to do it without supervision. If she does her homework most of the time but misses an assignment occasionally, your trust isn't lost, but you'll expect an explanation and will check up on her more often. And if she habitually fails to complete assignments, you'll know that she needs close supervision while doing homework.

Likewise, if you consistently do well what you are assigned to do, and then one day you use an MMT to be more effective, even if your MMT is uncovered, rarely will it cause you any trouble. In fact, you may be rewarded for finding a tool to improve effectiveness.

Are you confident when you can use an MMT effectively? If you are confident using it, and you use it, you will know whether it worked or not. If it didn't work, don't use it again in that workplace. Be assured, rarely will anyone know you tried something new.

Are you using the MMT with right motives? Using a tactic with the right motive for an appropriate purpose prevents most problems, because the outcomes benefit all concerned.

The real questions is—who has the courage to use an MMT?

In all organizations, everyone faces challenges about what they should do. In any organization challenges exist: there are personal differences, people get angry at other people, regulations and rules inhibit progress, evaluation and reward systems are not applied equally, and much more. So why do more than you have to do?

Most people believe that organizational problems are not their problems, so they leave them for someone else to fix.

In my neighborhood, many residents and maintenance workers do not believe they should pick up other people's trash—sometimes even their own. As a resident, should I do something, or wait for someone else to do something?

There is another option—"If it is going to be (what's right), it's up to me." So now when I walk around the neighborhood, I pick up everybody's trash. Am I thanked for what I do? Rarely. Do people know who picks up their trash? A few. Should I care if I'm just doing what is right? I don't care, I believe in what that bracelet says: "WWJD." What Would Jesus Do?

Our answer is, if the MMT will help you do the right thing— DO IT!

CHAPTER THREE

What is a Right Purpose or Motive?

IN 1968, WHEN HE was a sophomore at Harvard College, Kent Keith wrote a booklet for high school student leaders titled *The Silent Revolution: Dynamic Leadership in the Student Council.* This booklet contained his "Paradoxical Commandments," which have since been widely circulated, paraphrased, and recirculated. Here are a few of them that apply to employees who want to do the right thing:

- People are illogical, unreasonable, and self-centered. Love them anyway.
- If you do good, people will accuse you of selfish ulterior motives. Do good anyway.
- The good you do today will be forgotten tomorrow. Do good anyway.
- Honesty and frankness make you vulnerable. Be honest and frank anyway.
- Give the world the best you have and you'll get kicked in the teeth. Give the world the best you have anyway.

One popular paraphrase, often misattributed to Mother Teresa, concludes with "For you see, in the end, it is between you and God—It never was between you and them anyway." (For the full list of paradoxical commandments and how they came to be associated with Mother Teresa, see Dr. Keith's website, paradoxicalcommandments.com.)

The point of these aphorisms is that worldly people's foibles can't stop you from doing the right thing.

Remember what my friend Rebecca told me—if the worst thing your organization can do is fire you, and you get fired for doing what is right, the sun will still come up tomorrow. You may even find yourself living a better life. By simply doing the right thing, like forgiving someone, you demonstrate your values to your fellow colleagues. As long as you are succeeding, people will wonder why everybody doesn't do what you are doing.

In two different nonprofit organizations, I tried to further our mission by collaborating with others who shared the same objectives as my organization. I was given permission to do this; however, at each organization, when a new president was elected, he was jealous of the attention I received. He thought he should get that attention, so he fired me.

Cindy believed God wanted us to start our own business. We did, and were very successful. Trust God to tell you what to do.

Doing the Right Thing Builds Trust

When using an MMT, it is important to have the right purpose or motive.

What is a right motive? We believe that if you can answer the following five questions with a *no*, the motive you have is right:

- Are you doing this to get rewarded or promoted?
- Are you doing this to boost your pride?
- Are you seeking revenge against people who have hurt you?
- Are you trying to show that your boss is incompetent?
- Are you usurping power that rightly belongs to someone else?

Why is it so important to have the right purpose or motive to use an MMT?

It is all about trust. Someone who trusts another person to do the right thing is willing to give that person more freedom and forgiveness than someone they don't trust.

For example, if you use the Double Cut Tactic (see Chapter Five) because you think your boss is incompetent and just wants to push his employees to do more for less, and he suspects you are using an MMT, it may backfire on you.

The key to successfully deploying an MMT is *trust*. Trust must be earned, and the easiest way to earn trust is doing the right thing. The easiest way to lose trust is doing the wrong things. Once trust is lost it is hard, sometimes impossible, to regain.

If you have an affair with someone outside your marriage, and your spouse discovers this, trust will be lost. During my marriage I have had to take many overnight trips to other cities with women colleagues. My wife trusted me to be good, so it was never an issue in our marriage.

A child may be afraid to walk on his own, but will do so if his dad holds out his hands to catch the child from falling. If the child trusts its dad, it will try to walk on its own.

In 2017, after a series of widely publicized complaints from employees and customers, Travis Kalanick, then CEO of a popular ride share company, brought in consultants to help the company rebuild the trust of its workers, customers, and shareholders. Ultimately those efforts were not enough to restore people's trust in Kalanick, and he eventually left the company.

One consultant, Frances X. Frei, worked with Kalanick's replacement, Dara Khosrowshahi, with a focus on rebuilding trust internally, in part by clarifying the company's values, using input from its 15,000 employees. In an article for *Harvard Business Review*, Frei and colleague Anne Morriss wrote that "The new motto they settled on was 'We do the right thing. Period.'"

Frei and Morriss note that within a year, the company had stabilized: "indicators such as employee sentiment, brand health, and driver compensation were all heading in the right direction" ("Begin with Trust," *Harvard Business Review*, May–June 2020).

When trust has been breached, it can take a lot of hard work to restore it. By focusing on doing the right thing, workers can build and maintain trust with management that will make the deployment of Manage Management Tactics easier.

CHAPTER FOUR

The Greatest MMT of All Time

Learn from the best and do it their way.

GOAT MEANS THE GREATEST Of All Time. It is the title given to the person who has excelled the most in their sport, profession, or other endeavor. For example, in American football, Tom Brady is the GOAT; in professional golf Tiger Woods is the GOAT, and in gymnastics Simone Biles is the GOAT.

Why is it important to identify who is the GOAT?

If you want to participate in that field or sport, you need to know who is the best, so you can model your game after that person. By doing so, you can improve your game. Many fans wear shirts bearing the GOAT's name or picture as inspiration to emulate them. If the GOAT recommends or designs equipment, many will buy that gear in hopes of replicating the GOAT's achievements.

Identifying the GOAT from the fifty MMTs in this book gives you the tactic that will provide you with the boost that will be most beneficial in helping you do the right thing.

Once I was assigned a seemingly impossible task at Kodak—to set up a computer audit function as part of the internal auditing department. Computer auditing was a new concept in the late 1960s, and Kodak's external auditors wanted us to implement it.

I had no idea what the overall mission was for computer auditing, much less knowing what specific actions were needed. I felt doomed to failure.

Nothing is impossible with God, so I asked God what should I do. The answer I got was to find out what others were doing in computer auditing, and then do the same at Kodak.

So that's what I did. I asked several organizations—Kodak's external auditors, IBM, the National Bureau of Standards (now the National Institute of Standards and Technology, part of the US Department of Commerce), and the American Institute of CPAs— who was best at computer auditing. They told me, I visited those places, and within months I was one of the best computer auditors in the world (a little bragging).

I needed a test plan; the NBS had it. I needed to know how to review a computer system being built; AT&T told me how.

This seems such a simple concept. Find out who is the best at what you need, and copy them. I wondered why more people did not use this technique. I later found out why. Many bosses and organizations harbor this myth: "If it was not invented here, it cannot be good."

The GOAT of Manage Management Tactics

You would probably be amazed if you counted up how often, in just one month, you asked others for the "best" of something.

What is a great Italian restaurant?

Would you go back and see that movie again?

What brand of frozen vegetables would they recommend?

Did you like the movie The Little Mermaid?

If you're having trouble setting up spreadsheets, why not ask someone in another department to help you?

If you're spending too long building test data, buy a testing book, Google a solution, or talk with someone you know in another company and ask them how they do it.

You will be surprised how willing people are to help you. And they feel important when they are asked for help. Do not try to work things out on your own if a solution is only a phone call away.

There are two conflicting principles in business. The first is, "If it wasn't invented here, it is probably no good." The second and conflicting principle is, "We want continuous process improvement."

In the early years of computer programming, the programmers believed using a process to build software hindered its development. That concept is now gone, thank goodness. It was proved to be costly and inefficient. However, many people still do not believe that following a process is the quickest way to do a job. For example, when you're assembling flat-pack furniture, do you read and follow the implementation instructions? Or do you wing it and only read the instructions when the item doesn't go together correctly?

Hence the expression, "When all else fails, read the directions."

Obviously, if employees do not believe in and follow processes, there is no need or opportunity for continuous process improvement. Organizations that believe in and follow processes, usually are willing to have their people find better ways to do their jobs.

When should you look for better ways to do your job? First, if you are looking for a simple recommendation that you can implement yourself, ask for advice. If you want to know the best software package for bookkeeping, ask for recommendations, then buy it and use it.

Second, if you cannot implement a solution yourself, ask for a process you can acquire and implement. Some solutions come from vendors, some from government or nonprofit agencies, and some from individuals.

You could ask for a software package that creates test data and find out how to use it, or you could look for a written process you can acquire and implement. When searching for a solution, be a specific as possible in describing what you need.

How can you find better ways to do your job? There is a saying, "Ask and it will be given to you." In my experience, people from one organization are willing to share processes with people in other organizations, as long as they are not direct competitors.

In the USA, the Freedom of Information Act requires federal agencies to share what they have with anyone in the country (barring classified information and other sensitive data, like personnel files). If there's an intersection between your company's work and a government agency, this can be a good place to start.

It has been said that over 90 percent of all the information in the world is accessible from an iPhone. Learn how to write effective search queries.

Your company's vendors and other contractors can usually tell you which of their customers may have what you were looking for. If so, get a referral to an individual in that company and call them.

In many fields, there may be user groups or professional associations you can join to meet others whose work is related to yours.

Something I did not do, but should have, is to update my contacts list and add a description of each person's specialty to their entry. The solution I need might already be in my address book.

Do you have to tell your manager where you get your ideas? No, but it might be advantageous to tell your manager *how* you got new ideas. Showing them you are proactive in seeking out solutions lets them know you are more concerned with improving quality than with getting promoted. However, usually both happen together.

Personally, I like to identify my sources, and if the idea is implemented, I'll tell my source and thank them for the help.

As a consultant, I often ask the workers in an organization that hires me what needs to be done. Then I write that up as my recommendation to management and am greatly rewarded for my work. Why doesn't a company listen to their own employees? Often the answer is, "Our subordinates are not smart enough to innovate" or "They have an ulterior motive." By filtering the workers' suggestions, I alleviate management's concerns.

Remember that the quickest and cheapest way to solve a problem is to find the answer from someone who already knows how to do it, and implement their solution.

CHAPTER FIVE

Tactics for Bypassing Roadblocks

Sometimes the only way to get things done is,
"If it's going to be, it's up to me."

A TURTLE KNOWS, WHEN danger is near, to stick their head back inside their shell until the danger passes. However, if the turtle wants to move, they must put their head outside their shell and risk being decapitated. The same is true in business. If you reach a point in your work where you are blocked, like the turtle you have two choices. First, pull your head into your shell and wait for someone else to get you out of your concern. Second, take the bull by the horns and pull yourself out of the mud.

If you're willing to play "you bet your job" and do what is needed, you will either be crowned a hero or will need to beg for forgiveness. If you were doing what is in the best interest of your organization, you will almost always be forgiven.

The MMTs in this section are designed to help those willing to stick their neck out to make the right things happen.

Captain Hopper did it when she could not get a senior officer to sign off on a needed project. She was forgiven. I did it when I took a job running an association, because I was told I could do some other things as long as the organization was successful. The organization grew fast, but I was warned not to do too much. I did as promised and still got fired.

Yes, there is a risk when you do what needs to be done without first getting management approval. I learned a lesson then: if you're too good at your job, you become a threat to your boss and coworkers.

I took the risk because if I could not make a difference in my work, I knew I would be happier and better off elsewhere. Most of today's younger workers feel the same way about work: they say the reward of doing meaningful work is more important to them than money.

 Many management policies and controls are good, for example, ensuring that federal and state laws are complied with, and keeping teams advised with meaningful status reports. However, many are designed to ensure poor workers work, for example, when employees are required to check in and out each day. This sends a message that when you start and stop work is more important than what you do or whether you do it well. It also says *I don't trust you*, which can lead good workers to mistrust managers in return.

Controls cost time and money and can hinder good workers from working. Some controls require management approval before workers can advance to the next step of a project. In addition, many supervisors do not like some of the controls they must live with, and when asked for approval they indiscriminately sign whatever their workers give them.

Good workers follow good controls designed to prevent prob-lems, but when controls hinder them from completing their proj-ects on time and within budget, MMTs are a good solution. The MMTs in this chapter are designed to help you bypass manage-ment roadblocks and do meaningful work.

It Is Easier to Get Forgiveness than Permission
Take the initiative to do the right thing.

There are many reasons managers don't give subordinates permission to do things that probably should be done. Giving permission might be a risk to the manager. The boss might not be available. A decision may need to be made quickly with no time available to ask for permission. The boss may want to stay safe and follow the book (if your boss does nothing, your boss cannot do anything wrong). The boss may be more interested in power and perks and unconcerned with the success of the project or even the organization.

If the subordinate believes an action in the best interest of the organization, it should be taken, and if the subordinate knows it's the right thing to do, it can be done. If the result is favorable, the manager will forgive the risk taker and probably thanks the subordinate for taking action, even without permission.

As mentioned in Chapter One, this strategy comes from Captain Grace Hopper of the U.S. Navy, an organization whose chain of command is rigid. She knew that when a superior does not recog-nize the negative ramifications of not taking action, someone should step up and do the thing.

If the action taken doesn't work, the manager is blameless, and what happens to the person who acted is up to their manager. In most cases, the manager will recognize why the person did it and forgive them. If it works, everyone is happy. Just as in families, where "if Momma is happy, everybody is happy."

Good workers—those who want their organization to succeed and will work to make that happen—may often find themselves in a situation where they know what to do but cannot get
permission to do what is needed.

In those instances, the worker has a decision to make: either
take no risks, wait for permission, or just do what your boss wants;
or to do what is in the best interest of your organization—do the
right thing.

If your organization is willing, when you are assigned a project, ask your boss what you are empowered to do during the life
of your project.

What should a subordinate consider in making a decision to
do something without permission?

First, in an emergency situation always do what is right.

Second, what are the consequences of not doing it? If the consequences are minor, it is best to wait and ask for permission. If the
consequences are significant, and you do not believe your boss will
approve it or your boss is not available, do what is in the best interest of your organization.

If you do something significant without permission, what are
the possible consequences? The positive consequences could range
from a pat on the back for doing something necessary, to an award
or bonus, to becoming a candidate for promotion. In many cases,
you'll be forgiven for doing what you thought was right. Depending
on your boss, you might also be reprimanded or told that what you
did will negatively affect your performance appraisal, you might be
told to only follow procedures from now on. Worst case, you may
be fired.

When you let possible negative consequences stop you from
acting, you are responsible for the consequences your organization might suffer by not doing the right thing. The cost to complete the project might go up, or schedules might be missed.

My friend Rebecca was a schoolteacher in the New York City
public education system. One day, a student bought a gun into the

classroom and shot at her. The student missed and ran away. After that, Revecca left public education and went into banking. She told me that from then on she would no longer be afraid to do the right thing for her bank, because the worst thing they could do was fire her, not kill her.

A worker once asked me, while his boss was away, if he could get an advance for his planned business trip in three days. I had no authority to approve his request, but his boss would not return from vacation until after his planned departure. I signed his request for an advance, giving my name and title. He got his money, but I worried what my consequences would be.

There were none.

Two months later, I was asked to approve overtime for a project leader whose boss was also away. That person did not work for me, but I gave her approval anyway. And again, no consequences.

I signed a few more approvals, and in time the staff in my department thought I was authorized to approve requests. How could this have happened? I was never sure, but I assumed that if my boss knew what I was doing he might've stopped me. However, I had nothing to gain personally, and only did what my boss probably would have done.

Within a year I was promoted.

Did my making the right decision without approval help me? I don't know, but I thank Captain Hopper anyway.

The 85/15 Principle
Spend 85 percent of your time working and 15 percent preparing for and finding your next job.

Most workers spend all their working hours working for their employer (we are not counting goof-off time). Many of my friends have been laid off (including me) with two weeks' notice, especially those working on a contract. Remember most companies' Golden Rule: "What is best for the company is what they will do."

Too many people are surprised, some depressed, others mad at being laid off with only two weeks' notice. They have no idea what to do. What they should have done is prepare for that day and when laid off, execute their freedom plan. We believe six hours per week will do it, which you can make up by eliminating coffee breaks, cutting down on chitchat with coworkers, and returning from lurch early.

Parkinsons's Law states that work expands to fill all the available time. Cyril Northcote Parkinson, a historian, developed this law after analyzing statistics published by the British Admiralty on its activities during the first quarter of the twentieth century. The study showed that although the number of ships in commission dropped from sixty in 1914 to twenty in 1928, the number of admiralty positions increased from 2,000 to 3,569. Since the study, it is generally accepted that people will use as much time as is available to do their jobs. According to Parkinson, if a worker has five hours available to do a job, he will take five hours to do the job even if it's possible to complete it in two hours.

Parkinson saw that work and time are not necessarily related. This means that neither you nor your performance is evaluated on the amount of work accomplished in a given time. An exception to this is piecework. In that case, workers are paid per item assembled. However, in most cases job security does not depend on output. As Parkinson saw in the British Admiralty, the volume of work can actually decrease, while the size of the staff increases. Yet everyone keeps busy doing the available work, whatever that may be.

How does Parkinson's law affect you? There is a short-term impact and a long-term impact.

In the long term, when management realizes that hiring more people did not affect their profits, they must decide what they should do. Often they use Parkinson's law in reverse. They lay off people, and find that a smaller group can do the same amount of work that the larger group did. If people have just been doing busy work, they have margin to pick up the work left by the laid-off staff.

In the short term, you have to find something to do after you have done your work but have time left. This is where the 85/15 tactic comes into play. Complete your assigned work in 85 percent of your time, leaving 15 percent of your time to act as your own public relations manager, press agent, and job placement manager.

Don't expect your boss to do that job for you. They are too busy spending 15 percent of their day trying to get more money for themselves and get promoted.

Now you have the task of bettering yourself by using 15 percent of your time for similar purposes. Consultants do this as a regular part of their work: they spent 85 percent of their time helping their clients and 15 percent of their time searching for their next job—hopefully at your organization.

If you want to be a good employee, how can you spend the time that you do not need to complete your work?

You can go to your boss, tell them you have completed all your work, and ask, "What can I do now?"

Does this make your boss happy? Not at all. First, they think you may be not be doing all you could to do quality work. Second, you have put your boss on the spot—now they have the task of finding more work for you to do, instead of doing their job. Your boss can't let you sit around doing nothing. So your boss tells you to go through all their files and throw out everything over three years old.

Welcome to busy work world. You asked for it—doing something you don't enjoy.

Instead, use your 15 percent margin to find your next assignment doing a job you *would* enjoy. You're much better off selecting your own future jobs than allowing your boss to come up with a busy work assignment.

Now you are probably asking yourself, why didn't I ever think about managing my own career? Perhaps your family told you all you had to do was work hard and be patient. Maybe your business school never mentioned you need to manage your own career.

What if, with all you have to do both at work and after work, you don't have the time to do that? The answer to all those questions is the 85/15 theory. To get some ideas watch the movie *How to Succeed in Business Without Really Trying.*

To manage your career, keep networking and learning. Here are some methods to employ:

- Create an address book of the people who you think can help you in the future.
- Tell your friends outside your company to keep a lookout for you about available jobs.

To develop your skills, try a combination of the following:

- Read business journals and other news sources to find out where the jobs are.
- Take advantage of any program your company offers that will pay your way to get more education.
- Get as many degrees and certifications as are available to you; some might be small, like a certification for a particular software.
- Your company may be required to post open jobs: keep watching for one you might like.
- Learn what other people do, both inside your company and at others.
- Read company manuals and those from vendors whose equipment or software you use regularly.
- Explore what manuals and white papers relevant to your business are available through the federal government; these are often freely available on agency websites.
- Search the internet for skills that are needed in your industry.
- Take courses online or through libraries, community colleges, and professional associations.
- Attend conferences in your industry (may require company approval).

• Explore learning options offered by your company.
• Search for ways to improve your job.
• Define your criteria for making a job move.

Managing your career is an important part of your job. Create time for this job by using the 85/15 principle. Don't expect results tomorrow; they will come as you keep looking, improving, and persevering.

Put a Man On the Moon
Everything is impossible until someone does it.

On May 25, 1961, in a speech to Congress, President John F. Kennedy said, "I believe this nation should commit itself to achieving the goal, before this decade is out, of landing a man on the moon and returning him safely to earth."

How was this to be done? In 1961, the National Aeronautics and Space Administration had only flown one manned rocket flight: that of Astronaut Alan B. Shepard Jr. aboard *Freedom 7*, a Mercury Redstone launch vehicle.

It fell to NASA to assemble their best people to spearhead Project Apollo. Many people volunteered, but only a few were chosen. To screen the many applicants, managers listed all the tasks that needed to be done, and selected the hardest of them for the first challenge. Their thinking was that if the applicants couldn't solve the hardest task, testing them on the others would be a waste of time.

If there is no known solution for what you're asked to do, you will have to get help from other people. If the challenge carries a high probability of failure, why would you, like the NASA engineers, want to take it on?

Think about how the NASA engineers must have felt when they sent men to the moon and returned them safely. That could be you and your company. Also think how much recognition the

NASA engineers on Project Apollo received after the mission was complete.

American people love the home run in baseball, the breakaway in hockey, the knockout in boxing, and when good triumphs over evil. We shout "shoot for the moon" when we have nothing to fear but fear itself.

How can an impossible task be accomplished? Remember that the Bible says all things are possible with God; you will need God to put you in contact with those who can help you meet the challenge. We will explain how later.

In one sense, overcoming seemingly impossible odds is easy. All that is needed is to overwhelm obstacles with resources. Damn the torpedoes, full speed ahead.

But putting a man on the moon was not easy—it took dedicated people, resources, work, and more resources, hope and resources, and more and more resources. The American people never doubted that putting a man on the moon was "impossible." They just believed that with enough resources we could overcome the impossibility.

What is important to remember is that management really believes that anything is possible in any timeframe if they allocate enough resources to it. Let's look at a scene that illustrates management's viewpoint.

One Friday afternoon, Bill's boss asks Bill to have a special report available for him at nine o'clock Monday morning.

Bill answers, "There just isn't enough time to complete the report by Monday morning. I don't have enough people. I'm sorry, but it cannot be done."

What do you think Bill's boss thinks when he hears Bill's response? The boss knows anything is possible with enough resources, so when Bill says it cannot be done, his boss thinks Bill must be incompetent. Apparently, Bill doesn't understand "putting a man on the moon."

Bill's boss knows his manager needs that report Monday morning to present to a board meeting. Before consulting with Bill, he promised his manager the report would be ready: "What time do you need it?"

Bill's boss knows the "putting a man on the moon" tactic.

What Bill should have said was, "I can do it, but I will need three people to help me, plus your secretary all weekend." Bill says this so his boss will know exactly what resources are needed to accomplish Bill's mission.

If it is very important to get the report done by Monday, Bill's boss will approve the personnel and overtime pay. If it's not that important, Bill's boss might delay the meeting until Tuesday or Wednesday.

When I began working in the consumer department of Kodak in the early 1960s, they had an IBM 705 computer. Kodak wrote their own compilers, so they only needed one compiler for the IBM 705. Then Kodak bought several IBM 1401 computers. Now their programmers needed a compiler that could output software for either computer.

I was assigned this project to "put a man on the moon," meaning write one compiler a programmer could use that would work on whichever computer they planned to use. My compiler was to be called Multicoder, and it would be the first compiler in the world that could do what my compiler would do.

My instructions were to determine how to do it, estimate the resources I would need, get them, and go to work. If I needed more resources, I could get them with no questions asked.

I completed my mission in four months.

Here are the steps to employ the Put a Man on the Moon Tactic:

1. Get agreement that what you are being asked to do is impossible unless you get the necessary resources. Management knows nothing is impossible, so they may downplay the difficulty of what you're being asked to do. If so, say something

like, "If our competition does this first, we could be in real trouble." Or, "What could be more important than what you are asking me to do?" or "If we pull it off we will all be promoted," or "If anybody could do it we can."

2. Agree to do it *only* if you get *all* the resources necessary.
3. If you don't have enough resources, never say you cannot do it, but tell management you underestimated the resources needed, and ask for more.

As a worker, you must understand the way management thinks and use it to your advantage if you want to enhance your career.

The Double Cut
By doubling your request for funding,
you can double the fun.

The Double Cut Tactic has been standard procedure in home and business since time immemorial. When you were a child (subordinate) you asked for four dollars a week allowance, and your parents (management) gave you two. When you asked to stay out until midnight, you got to stay out until ten o'clock. Then you got out of school and went to work. Perhaps no one told you, but the same principle applies there.

You ask for different things from different managers, but their cuts do you in. You request $500 to attend a vital seminar. Your request is cut in half, and you're told to find a seminar closer to headquarters to save travel costs, and so forth.

Your department budgets are cut, your orders for supplies are cut, and the staff members assigned to your project are cut. The only thing that is never cut is the number and scope of the tasks you're asked to perform. If you don't know the Double Cut Tactic, it's time you did. It can work to your advantage.

Many managers are concerned that their employees are not committed to doing what they are asked to do on time and within budget. Therefore, managers believe subordinates will ask for more help with the project, more time to do the project, and more money for the project than they need. Many managers feel they are only doing their job by cutting subordinates' requests down to what is, in the manager's mind, reasonable. If you have such a boss, ask for what you need, plus the amount by which you think your boss will cut your request so you get what you really need. Management can make its cut and yet your project can still be completed.

In any workplace, there are those who get ahead and those who fall behind. In many cases, the ones who fall behind do so because they do not understand and use the Double Cut Tactic. They ask for only what they need, and get half that. So their projects are late and over budget. Those who get ahead ask for twice what they need and get half, which is exactly what they need. Their projects are on time and within budget. They are happy, and so are their managers.

Here's an example. It is all too typical, as you will discover, if you have not already.

Harvey was asked to put on a conference for the regional sales team. He picked a top-notch location and negotiated a rock-bottom price that would still allow him to put on a first-class event.

He sent his budget to the boss for approval. Knowing he would be expected to minimize costs, the boss cut a lot out of the proposal.

When Harvey got the approved budget back, he was depressed. He went back to the drawing board, changed the location to a second-tier venue, reduced the budget for the meals and the open bar, and gave up the entertainment.

You can imagine what happened. The sales team members were upset at the location of the event, the sub-par meals, the cash bar, and the lack of entertainment. Instead of being encouraged and inspired by the event, they griped about the cheapness of the company.

And what happened to Harvey? Despite his cost-cutting, he still overran his budget and faced the wrath of his boss, who had sunk a fine proposal with a stroke of his red pen.

The following year, a new chair was chosen for the event. She knew the Double Cut Tactic, so she doubled the amount she asked for and got what she needed.

The sales team left that year's conference with enthusiasm, and the new chair was rewarded.

Rarely is a budget request approved as submitted. This happened to me in an unexpected way. For a meeting I was running, I asked for twice what I needed, and then got what I asked for! What to do with the extra money?

I upgraded the meeting in many ways, and the attendees said it was the best event they had ever attended. Of course I also got the attaboy from the boss.

There are some simple lessons to be learned.

1. Always ask for twice as much as you need on the assumption that your boss will cut your request in half.
2. In the long run management will remember your successes, not the real cost of the project.
3. The Double Cut Tactic allows your manager to fulfill his function of cutting out the fat without destroying the operation.
4. The Double Cut Tactic does not always have to be asking for twice what you need. If you know your boss only cuts 25 percent, adjust your request accordingly.

The Double Cut Tactic belongs in everyone's repertoire. Use it wisely, and only when appropriate, but use it.

A Dead Fish Stinks from the Head Back
It is easier to see the effect of something bad
than to determine the cause.

I was an examiner for the Malcolm Baldridge National Quality Program, which developed seven criteria to define a world-class management system. The role of the examiner was to numerically score how close each organization's management system compared to the program's criteria.

For example, here are the components of one criterion—leadership:

1. How the organization's vision and values were deployed throughout their organization
2. How management promoted an environment that fostered and required legal and ethical behavior
3. How management created an organization that would be sustainable for years
4. How management communicated with, empowered, and motivated employees at all levels
5. How management created a focus on accomplishing the organization's objectives, improved performance, and strived to achieve the organization's vision

Management that does these things creates an environment in which employees are motivated to work hard, do whatever is needed to improve processes, and enjoy coming to work each day. What I learned as a consultant is that employees rarely leave an organization for more money; they leave because of poor management. When managers only do a few of these things, their organization begins to die at the top, and slowly their organization starts to stink.

How can you tell when management, at the top or elsewhere in the organization, starts to die or perhaps is already dead? Poor management is defined by different people in different ways. Auditors use large turnover of staff. The stock market uses earnings per share and stock price. Workers use micromanaging, which means their boss doesn't trust them or doesn't want them to take initiative.

Customers measure their dissatisfaction by how they are treated, not only when they first come into contact with an employee from the organization they are buying from, but also when they have a complaint or need to return merchandise. They also judge the availability of management and frequency of communication.

As a Baldrige examiner, I would ask workers questions about their leadership:

- What is the mission of your organization?
- How often do you see your boss?
- What types of communication do you receive from upper management?
- Does your organization have an open-door policy so you can communicate with anyone in management?

When employees lack knowledge about their organization, that indicates a communication problem. A great example of a successful CEO was Fred Smith at Federal Express. Among the many noteworthy things he did was that each day he posted key statistics, available to all employees, about the company, such as how many packages were delivered on time.

My daughter worked for a nonprofit organization. She was highly skilled at her job as a meeting planner and received many "well done" compliments from attendees. She was very innovative and did new things to make her meetings exciting to attend. In my opinion, her boss was a micromanager, and was jealous of her success. He took a dislike to her, and made her look like poison to her coworkers so they would not talk to her and would not have lunch with her.

Then her boss built a case, based on lies, to fire her. Fortunately, she had evidence to disprove the lies. The CEO of the organization only did things that made him look good and did not care how his subordinates treated those that worked for them.

When her boss fired her, she went to human resources and showed how he had lied about her. They knew she had a strong legal case, so they made her a generous settlement. The CEO didn't care she was fired falsely and kept her boss.

What is the moral of the story? When the top dog in an organization doesn't care about the welfare of the employees, as they say in dog racing, the dogs that follow can only see the dog in front of them and just keep following the lead dog.

The question good employees need to ask is *what can I do if I have a bad boss?*

Some employees decide to wait until their bad boss is fired, transferred, or quits. In some organizations where I have taught new technology, I was told by attendees they wished they could use the new technology, but they had to wait until they got a new boss. Some employees try to get transferred to a new boss. Others, especially those who need the job, just keep rolling along, hoping things will get better.

If the bad boss is your boss, learn all you can, take courses to improve yourself, and look for a better job in your organization. If the stink comes from a higher level, there is a little hope for a good employee. In my case, I looked for a new job, and the one I got was much better than the one I left.

Change the Name, Change People's Attitude
If there is something you do not like, change its name.

In the movie *The Blind Side*, the football player did not like his nickname Big Mike, so he changed it to Michael. People often change their names, either through marriage or adoption or for other reasons. Names are important.

President Kennedy wanted to compete with the Soviet Union, but rather than ask for funding for a space race, which might be controversial, he set a goal of putting a man on the moon by the end of the decade, and asked for funds to achieve the goal. NASA got all the money it needed.

After Flight 592 crashed in the Everglades in 1996, its cut-rate airline negotiated a merger with a much smaller company, which was part of a large parent company. After the merger, the cut-rate airline changed its name to that of the large parent company, a brand which lacked the negative publicity the airline had picked up after the crash.

This theory is so common and effective in the real world, we wonder why it is not used within more organizations. If you have unhappy employees, a very difficult project, or something that might fail for lack of support, consider changing the name of your problem.

Changing a title can turn failure into success. A carrier service using runners in New York City to move financial documents from place to place had a high turnover rate and poor morale. After analysis, the problem turned out to be that the runners felt their jobs were unimportant. To remedy this, the carrier service changed the name *runner* to *transfer agent*. Problem solved.

You might argue that the Change the Name Tactic only works for things highly visible to the public, but it can work just as well in a small department. Programmers became motivated by changing *data processing* to *information technology*. Employees in *personnel* departments were motivated by changing the name to the *human resources*. People testing software like to be called *quality assurance specialists*. People called *supervisors* like *manager* much better.

So renaming a job, a department, a task, or a project can all contribute to motivating workers. This MMT can bring about significant changes in your workplace, just by changing names.

CHAPTER SIX

MMTs for Successful Negotiating

Negotiating means conferring, bargaining,
or discussing with two or more people with
a goal of reaching agreement.

IN BUSINESS, GOVERNMENTAL RELATIONSHIPS, and marriage, there will be a consistent, constant stream of disagreements. There is a wrong way and a right way to settle disagreement. The wrong way is trying to exert your will over another person, whether by shouting, fighting, separation, divorce, or warfare. Or, as they say in the army, "If you fight and run away, you live to fight another day." The right way is through negotiating. If you choose negotiating, be prepared to compromise, so you can achieve a win-win situation. Normally neither party will get all they want, but each will get something that is acceptable to them. Who does this? Property brokers, family courts, and the US Congress.

Very few people have been trained in negotiating, but most people negotiate every day. We negotiate with too many parties to list, but some examples include parents, children, teachers, friends, colleagues, and bosses.

How do we do this without training? It seems natural, because we start negotiating with our parents at a very young age about what we will eat, when we will go to bed, how we can get toys, and much more. When we enter teenage years, the negotiating get much more serious as we rebel against our parents' authority. Negotiation continues throughout our lifetime.

Without training, the negotiation tricks we learn are ineffective ones like yelling, crying, punishing, walking away, and divorce. We learn these tricks by experimentation that tells us which tricks work on which people.

However, there are effective negotiating rules and practices which, when used, will eliminate much of the stress and anger and help you reach a settlement much sooner.

The rules primarily define what topics will or will not be included in a negotiation. For example, "We will not discuss past events or our feelings about everything involved, and we will follow the rules of good behavior."

Here are some of the best negotiating practices:

- Determine what you want and how much you will be willing to compromise.
- Practice what you will say.
- Identify the key points you want to emphasize and focus your conversation on those key points.
- Do not disclose all the arguments you have for winning. Rather, save something to give up if you need to.

If you're not familiar with sales strategy, read books about it, such as *To Sell Is Human* by Daniel H. Pink or *Selling 101* by Zig Ziglar.

Tactics for Evading Not Invented Here Syndrome
What to do when only your boss's own ideas
are acceptable.

Where do new ideas originate? Almost everywhere.

How do new ideas get implemented? That depends.

In an ideal workplace, a new idea would be evaluated on the benefits it provides to the organization, the employees, and the customers. The more of those parties it benefits, the more likely the idea is to be implemented.

But too often new ideas don't get implemented.

In some cases, although the idea may be a good one, instead of evaluating it based on its benefit to stakeholders, it is evaluated based on where it came from and whether the evaluator believes the source is even capable of having good ideas.

In other cases, the person, organization, or department authorized to approve the new idea may believe they have a better idea, or believe the new idea can't work.

Both of these obstacles derive from NIH—"Not Invented Here" Syndrome—in which anything from outside the department or organization is immediately identified as inferior and therefore unacceptable.

The subconscious biases that produce NIH Syndrome may include a personal dislike for the originator of the idea, a suspicion that the person proposing the idea has a vested interest in its implementation, or a belief that the manager might look bad for not having suggesting the same idea earlier.

Be warned: NIH Syndrome can kill ideas, threaten the boss, and harm the organization if it isn't circumvented. Let's look at what NIH Syndrome looks like in action.

A talented meeting planner ran meetings based on lessons learned in her many years of experience, and she got great reviews. But her boss felt she was "out of control," doing things without his permission. He pulled an after the fact NIH by telling her she could not vary from his standard procedures for meetings without getting his approval first—which he never gave. What raises he gave her were inadequate. She lost her motivation and left the organization.

A low-level subordinate proposed to his boss an idea to improve the effectiveness of his work. The boss used NIH to cancel the idea, because she believed the subordinate had "a vested interest in having his idea approved."

The most common NIH is when, rather than developing an idea themselves, an employee finds the new idea elsewhere—reading about it in a trade journal, bringing it from a previous workplace, or learning it from a friend in another company. These imported ideas are often immediately rejected, under the theory that if the idea were any good, the manager, department, or company would already have developed it themselves.

Some bosses just want to keep the status quo, so they reject most ideas using a typical NIH response, such as, "We tried that, or something similar, and it didn't work." Too many times, NIH is deployed because if the new idea is effective, it will harm the boss's ego. If a boss feels he and his organization are already one of the best in the world at what they do, then the probability of improving their performance by implementing someone else's idea is, in his opinion, slim or none.

NIH Syndrome can literally destroy an organization, and this has happened too often. Perhaps the best example is Kodak. They were the worldwide leader in film technology, and film sales provided most of the company's income. Kodak also had one of the world's best research organizations, where in 1975 Steven Sasson built the first portable digital camera. When the research team presented the idea of digital photography to Kodak management, the film division thought that idea could kill their film sales. NIH Syndrome stopped Kodak from making and selling digital cameras and storage media. Instead of killing film sales, I feel NIH killed the entire company.

If your bosses suffer from NIH Syndrome, how can you circumvent them and get your idea accepted? Here are three ways:

1. Convince your boss that he or his boss talked about the idea some time ago and you just now figured out how to implement *his* idea. Of course, this way the boss will get all the credit, but at least your idea will get implemented.
2. Wait a few months, then suggest the idea under a different name (see "Change the Name") and give it a slightly different description.
3. Get someone else to suggest the idea. This is especially effective it it's someone who is evaluating your work processes, like a consultant. Again, you won't get the credit, but you will get the benefits of the idea's implementation.

Identify Areas of Improvement
If you're digging a hole and are getting nowhere,
stop digging.

One definition of insanity is doing the same thing repeatedly while expecting different results. If the thing you are doing is not producing the best results, and you keep doing it, you might as well be crazy.

The objective of this strategy is to identify when something you're doing isn't working as well as it could, stop doing it, and develop a better process. A sure way to keep doing something that does not work is to insist *we have always done it that way*.

To use this tactic you must do two things:

1. Identify a process that is not as effective or efficient as you would like.
2. Innovate a better process.

Sometimes this is easy. If your process pushing water to a lake through a four-inch pipe, and you believe your throughput could be improved, you could survey the pipeline. If your investigation shows that along the line it changes to a three-inch pipe then back to a four-inch pipe, it is easy to determine where the bottle-neck is. Once you know the cause of the problem, it's easy to fix.

Is this type of problem unique? No, it's just that people are not aware when something that seems to be working might have an opportunity for improvement. If you have always limped, that will seem normal to you, even though other people don't. But you think limping is the way you were built. However, if one leg is shorter than the other, that may be the problem. Then by putting a one-inch sole on the shorter leg's shoe, you can walk without a limp. People may go through life believing their handicap can't be fixed, but often it can.

Whose job is it to find a defect in a process? Usually no one, unless your organization has a "process improvement process." Who knows what processes need improvement? Usually, the people who use the process as part of their job.

I told you earlier that as a consultant I just had to ask workers what is stopping them from being more productive. They could almost always tell me. Why don't they tell their bosses?

Usually, it's because the boss doesn't believe the workers are smart enough to know, or the boss just wants them to get their job done and doesn't want to spend time on process improvements. It could also be that the boss doesn't want to hear complaints or bad news.

For example, in a computer system, the same type of error occurred frequently. When that particular error occurred, the error was flagged and given to a clerk to correct. As a consultant, when I asked that clerk how her job could be simplified, she said, "Stop this type of error from occurring so often." She kept records for herself, and handed me a two-inch file recording instances of that type of error. I asked why she said nothing to her boss. She said she thought her job was to correct errors.

Is this common? Yes. Let's look at how this tactic can help you save money in your home. How often is a light left on when no one is in the room? Do you heat the whole house while you're sleeping with your bedroom temperature lowered? How much food do you buy and not eat? What clothes do you buy and rarely wear? How much money do you give your children to waste? These are all opportunities to save.

Doing what does not work, or which works inefficiently, wastes money. You may have to continue using what's available to finish your job one time. But using that same wasteful process the next time meets the definition of insanity.

Let's look at two common missed opportunities that you may know about, but don't fix.

First, we know that when a potential customer goes to your website, if they cannot find what they want in three clicks they leave.

Second, if your staff doesn't answer the phone or respond quickly to emails, you may lose business.

Let's ask the question again: who is responsible to find a defect in a process? There is a widely known statement that many know but few act on: "If it's going to be, it's up to me."

If you know something needs to be fixed, and you don't act on it, you will have missed two opportunities: to help your organization, and to make you look good to your manager. Recommending ways to improve your organization is one of the best ways you can draw attention to your capabilities.

Lead a Horse to Water
Many great ideas never see the light of day because management will not approve them.

I have witnessed wonderful ideas, both large and small, fall by the wayside due to lack of management support. As the saying goes, you can lead a horse to water, but you can't make it drink. And you can give a manager a great idea, but you can't make them implement it.

In some cases, companies have gone bankrupt because management didn't understand the need for change. As noted earlier,

Eastman Kodak invented digital photography but decided not to pursue it.

In another case, one popular, national, box home furnishing store lost a lot of business to their competitors because they initially decided not to do business online. The owners thought people would rather shop in the store.

I once managed an association designed to help CPAs switch from paper tax preparation to computerized tax preparation. Those that did not switch lost business to the firms using the new technology.

Three questions must be answered if the horse is going to drink the water:

1. If you were a turtle would you stick your neck out, knowing a predator might kill you, to do whatever is necessary to sell your great idea?
2. What are the risks if your great idea is not accepted?
3. How can you persuade management to implement a great idea?

When I was a supervisor, many workers came to me with their great ideas. If I thought they were offering me the idea so I could do the work of implementation, which I did not have time or inclination to do, I would reject the idea. If they were serious about their idea, they would argue for approving their idea and take the initiative to implement it themselves. I'm sure the majority of ideas presented to management are not approved because the presenter failed to say, "If you approve my idea, I will work hard to make it happen."

Courage is necessary to get management to reconsider a rejected idea—unfortunately this is a trait many people do not have.

Kodak was presented with the idea of making a major effort to market digital photography. There must've been huge opposition from the film division, which produced most of the company's profits. Management would have had to override the wishes of the film division and kill Kodak's profit-making sacred cow. No one seemed to have the courage to do so.

How can you present a risk analysis that describes the risk of rejecting your idea? Obviously, Kodak's research division just presented the idea. They did not present the risk that would follow rejection: accepting their idea risked losing the film division, but rejecting the idea risked bankruptcy as the photography industry moved to digital production. Remember if you present small risks, your idea may still be rejected. If you present big risks, the probability of success increases.

For example, a company wanted to use an idea from dog kennels that permitted the dog owner to view their dog during the day. They wanted to sell this idea to childcare facilities, so parents could watch their children during the day. How could they present that idea to management? The risk of implementation included the risk that costs to parents might be so high they wouldn't pay for the service, and the project would fail. If daycare centers did not want to pay to install the needed equipment, the project would fail. But there was also the possibility that this would be one of the best ideas ever, and by not pursuing it they risked missing out on a large potential profit.

Once management knows the risks, how do you persuade them to accept those risk and implement your idea? Pastor Robert Schuller of the *Hour of Power* TV show wanted to build a Crystal Cathedral and did it by not giving the architects a budget but rather telling them that if they created the right cathedral, the money would come. And it did. As in the movie *Field of Dreams*, about building a baseball diamond in a corn field, "If you build it, they will come."

The best way to sell an idea is to sell the vision and assure management about what you can control during implementation, rather than who will buy it or use it. The company that wanted to use the kennel approach for daycare centers needed to sell a vision rather than the technical aspects of the system. The vision was transparency and trust. The transparency allowed the parents to see their children any time during the day they wanted to, and by seeing them, they could trust the daycare center to take care of their children. It is "trust but verify." The vision sold, and the project was very successful.

This tactic requires you to do three things to get the horse (management) to drink:

1. Have the courage to, as Winston Churchill often preached, "never give up"—keep fighting until management gives up.
2. Explain to a manager the risks of rejecting your idea.
3. Sell the vision, not the technical aspects.

Keep Your Ace In The Hole
Negotiation is a process—not an art.

If you want to paint a picture on canvas you have two choices:

1. Use a process. Buy a "paint-by-number" outline of the picture with each piece telling you what color to paint that piece.
2. Paint as an artist, sitting at a blank canvas trying to decide what picture to paint.

Negotiating is a process—you do not have to make it up as you go.

In fact, it is a mistake to go into negotiations without preparation. The amount of time you spend preparing and the type of preparation, depends on the seriousness of what you are negotiating. Here are the key elements of most recommended negotiating processes:

Step One: Define specifically what you are negotiating about.

Step Two: Define exactly the minimum settlement you are prepared to accept.

Step Three: Prepare for, and rehearse, your arguments for settlement.

Step Four: Keep your ace in the hole—an offer to make after your best offer.

Step Five: Conduct the negotiation.

Step Six: Once you have gotten what you want, stop.

Using an example of negotiating the purchase price of a new automobile may help you understand this process.

Start by knowing which automobile you want and the price the dealer is asking, and then turn down the offer. Determine the most you will pay, and if the dealer offers the car at that amount or less, you buy. If the dealer makes a counter-offer for more than you want to pay, agree to that amount only if the dealer will accept your ace in the hole, which might be an upgrade the paint or tires.

Lastly, keep in mind that the person you are negotiating with may be very good at reading your nonverbal signals. Remember to maintain your poker face throughout the negotiation.

CHAPTER SEVEN

MMTs for Avoiding Quicksand

When trying to hurry, you can get trapped in quicksand; then your short cut becomes a long trip.

MANAGEMENT POLICIES ARE OF two types: those that help and those that hurt. Complying with federal payroll laws helps keep your company on track. Requiring workers to clock in and out hurts productivity because it shows management doesn't trust workers. Good employees are punished to keep bad workers working.

Too many policies are developed because management thinks more severe controls make poor employees more effective. But quality control principles state that if you do not trust employees, fire them. That is cheaper than developing an entire control system to control poor employees. Such control systems inhibit good employees from being efficient and effective. In other words, such systems are planting quicksand on the road to progress.

Micromanaging happens when a boss does not trust a subordinate to do a proper job. A micromanager will want regular reports to ensure that the workers do exactly what the boss wants them to do. Most workers being micromanaged feel they are being impeded from doing their job with creativity and innovation. They also learn that the way their boss wants things done is the only right way. If an employee varies from the way their boss wants, they will be subject to poor performance reviews.

Supervisors usually micromanage for three reasons:

1. The manager is insecure and fears the staff will do harm if not properly supervised.
2. The manager doesn't trust their staff to work hard.
3. The manager fears that if their staff is too good, they could take the micromanager's job.

Micromanagers have a habit of giving creative and innovative subordinates bad reviews, and in extreme cases may terminate an employee who varies too much from what the micromanager believes is the correct way to do work. If a subordinate follows whatever their boss wants, without be allowed to innovate, they become demotivated. There is no easy way to work with a micromanager, but these five tactics may help:

1. Do exactly what they tell you to do, and do it their way even if it makes you hate working for a micromanager.
2. Innovate in ways that will not easily be noticed.
3. Ask to be transferred to a job that isn't micromanaged job.
4. Quit your job and look for a better one.
5. Propose that your work be done by the PDCA Process (Plan, Do, Check, Act—see Chapter Eight) which uses independent people to check your work.

Coworkers can also use quicksand to make good workers look bad. Some people may resent a colleague because they think that person got something they should have gotten, such as a promotion or recognition. When that person sits on a committee run by the colleague they resent, they will do everything possible to hinder the project. They will try to monopolize committee meetings by suggesting different ways to do the project, objecting to the direction the project is going, arguing with other committee members, and instigating gossip to discredit the project leader. They try to delay the project to make the project leader look bad.

Supervisors, micromanagers, and resentful workers can all plant quicksand in your path. When that happens, you'll need deal with it. If a supervisor created the quicksand, find a supportive manager and solicit their help in circumventing the obstacle. If a coworker is planting quicksand, meet with them and ask them to let you manage the project without interference. If you must deal with it personally, the MMTs in this chapter will help you.

The Fudge Factor
If the probability of an overrun or underrun could cause a problem, add or subtract a fudge factor.

Estimates are sacred amounts to managers; they must be met. An estimate is just an estimate, but for customers and managers the estimate is what they expect to pay, or reward a subordinate, for a completed job. Too often estimates, budgets, schedules, and quotas are assigned by management for workers to achieve. Even when workers develop the figures, they are derived from rules laid down by management. That is why estimates, budgets, schedules, and quotas are a plague to workers. That is also why the fudge factors may be the only defense workers have to satisfy management.

Following is the Fudge Factor Formula:

Estimated Amount +/– Fudge Factor = Actual Amount.

Let's look at a business situation in which the subordinate does not understand the Fudge Factor Formula.

Fred is in charge of three projects, each with a budget of $10,000, for a total of $30,000:

Project A winds up with a 10 percent overrun, costing $11,000. Project B ends up costing 30 percent less, costing only $7,000. Project C ends up with a 20 percent overrun, costing $12,000.

The net result is that Fred completes all three projects for a combined cost of $30,000. Does Fred's boss think he did a good job? Of course not. Two of Fred's jobs were out of control and came in over budget. The conclusion is that Fred is a poor project manager.

Fred's problem is that he doesn't use the fudge factor.

Since fudge factors are so important, you need to understand how they work. They are adjustments, plugs, unknown factors, and similar items that cause the actual amounts to equal estimated amounts. Engineers, accountants, and purchasing agents have been using fudge factors for centuries.

There are two schools of thought about fudge factors. One says that fudge factors should be built into the estimated amount beforehand. This means if you think you can complete a project for $10,000, you add a fudge factor of 20 percent, making your estimate $12,000. This changed estimate allows for inflation, mistakes, or poor craftwork. If you think you can sell four hundred items, you estimate sales at three hundred, which is a fudge factor of one hundred items. You have just allowed for a recession, an unforeseen illness, or poor salesmanship.

The second school of thought on fudge factors says you begin with a realistic estimate, and add fudge factors as the date of reckoning approaches. The fudge factor must be appropriate for the situation. Fred shifted costs between accounts. Engineers and accountants specialize in this. Salesmen hold back sales and turn them in during critical periods when they fail to meet established quotas.

The beauty of the fudge factor is that, when you use it, you are virtually assured of success because you have hedged or fudged your bets. Management loves subordinates who consistently bring projects in under budget or consistently exceed quotas. Use the fudge factor and you will be loved by your manager.

Let's examine some fudge factor techniques so you will have several choices to choose from when the occasion occurs.

Underestimate Fudge: Deliberately underestimate a quota so it is easy to achieve.

Overestimate Fudge: When submitting cost estimates or schedules, add a factor, for example 20 percent, to be sure you don't over-run your budget or miss your scheduled completion date.

Plug Fudge: If some detail causes the total to be over budget or exceed the control amount, plug in the difference so it reconciles. For example, if one line item causes the project to be over budget, cut back on another line item.

Next Year Fudge: If sales or costs or income are not what they should be, shift them from one accounting period to the another. For example, if you have not met your sales goal, ask your best customer to place an order before year-end for delivery as needed. You hit your sales goal, your customer may get the purchase in before prices increase, and your sales manager is happy. This technique can also be used to over-purchase supplies, to spend money you might lose if it goes unspent at the end of the year. If you are on a cash basis, you can wait to deposit a check until next year while backdating the expense to this year.

Quality Fudge: If you can't adjust the price, plug the difference, or shift the cost, you can always change the quality. This is a very effective fudge. For example, if budgeted funds are not available to buy new equipment, you can buy used equipment. If funds don't allow you to pay for three coats of paint, you can get two. Engineers and builders use this fudge often, especially on fixed-cost projects. But exercise caution: the Titanic may have used this fudge.

These fudge factors are the worker's friend. While the ethics of some of these fudges may be questionable, they work. If you need them to avoid the methods management uses to evaluate you, and you think it is in the best interest of your employer, use them. Ask for forgiveness when necessary. Even if you decide not to use them, you need to understand them.

Garbage In, Garbage Out
Unless you fix your input, don't expect quality output

GIGO—Garbage in, garbage out—is an old computer term meaning that if the input is incorrect, the output will be incorrect. For example, if the number of hours an employee worked is incorrectly entered into the payroll system, the paycheck for that employee will be wrong.

This GIGO concept affects almost everything you do in life. If people keep saying that you can never get into a college, and you believe them, then you will never get into a college. If you believe garbage inputs, they can change your life for the worse.

Let's examine some of the many ways garbage in produces unsatisfactory results:

- You ask your child to clean up their room. To them that means get everything out of sight, while you meant put things away in drawers or the closet.
- If you believe you are a loser because other people tell you so, you can only be a loser.
- If you are offered a deal that seems too good to be true, it probably is.
- If you go to a grocery store without a shopping list, you will probably come home without everything you wanted.
- If you buy a suit at a bargain store expecting it to last as long as a suit from a top-notch clothing store . . . it won't.

What are all these examples trying to show? Don't let garbage past the starting gate.

If you have ever watched a tall building under construction, it will seem to take forever to build the foundation, but once that is done, the rest of the building goes up quickly. Why does the foundation take so long? Because if they don't get the foundation right, they will end up building the Leaning Tower of Pisa. If you want to build a home, and start building before the plans are complete, you will probably end up do a lot of re-work.

How can you tell garbage inputs from what is really wanted? The answer is simple: define the end product before you start building.

In a restaurant, if you ask your server for a nice steak dinner, you may expect a steak that's red in the center. The chef sends a steak that is raw in the center. It is still red. What happened? You didn't specify what you wanted so that you and the chef had the same definition of the end product.

Is it easy to define the end result you want? Sometimes yes, and sometimes no.

If you have a shopping list and check off each item as you put it in the cart, that's your picture. If a football team is losing because they don't know which of their plays are ineffective, they will need data analytics to get the scoreboard result they want.

To best describe the picture of what you want, do these three things:

1. Spend as much time as necessary to describe, in writing and pictures, what you want built, even if you are the builder. If you cannot describe the product you want, don't start building it. If you know a product similar to what you want, show it to the team who will develop your product. Until you have does this clear idea, don't start building the product.
2. Monitor product development regularly. This is called quality control. The cheapest way to assure you get what you want is to know what you want. The second way to minimize cost is to find and fix defects as soon as possible after they occur.
3. If what you are building is ready for delivery, or you are acquiring a completed product, examine it in detail to be sure it's what you want. For example, if you are buying an article of clothing, try it on before you buy it. Most importantly, before accepting delivery of the product, have the user test it to be sure it meets their quality standard.

To paraphrase what the Cheshire Cat said to Alice, if you don't know where you are going, any road will take you there. But many times you end up where you don't want to go. If you allow garbage in, you *will* get garbage out. That it is a self-fulfilling prophecy.

If You Don't Know How To Do It, Don't Try
The biggest mistake many people make is trying to do something they don't know how to do.

Too many people believe that admitting they don't know how to do something is a sign of incompetence.

Wrong.

A sign of incompetence is trying to do something you don't know how to do, and failing.

I used to get angry at my staff when I asked them to do something, and they would say something like, "Okay, Boss."

Then I would ask had they done it yet, and they might say, "Working on it."

I'd ask again and again until they said, "I need some help, Boss."

Then I'd say, "Why didn't you tell me you didn't know how to do it?"

They might reply, "I was hoping I could figure it out how to do it, and then do it for you."

Finally, my wife told me, "Before you ask someone to do something, you need to find out whether they know how."

Why wouldn't my employees admit they couldn't do what I asked?

They did not want to admit they couldn't do something that I considered them able to do.

I needed to ask myself a similar question. "Why do I expect my staff to be able to do anything I ask?

I know the answer to that question also. "My expectations are unrealistic." My conclusion is that in such cases, both the boss and the employees share the blame.

When you are asked to do something that you do not know to do, consider using one of these potential responses:

• I don't know how to do that now, but I'll find out how to do it, and then do it for you.
• If you know someone that knows how to do it, tell me, and I'll ask them to help me.
• I haven't been trained in that skill yet, but if you can tell me where to get the training, I'll be very appreciative. I'll learn that skill so I can do what you asked.

It is far better to be honest than to bluff.

The Blindside Tactic

Blindside is a football term meaning a right-hand passer can be hurt because he cannot see to his left.

If a right-handed quarterback cannot see someone coming from his left to hurt him, he is both vulnerable to being hit and in need of help to protect him. The person who can defend the passer's left side is one of the highest-paid players in professional football.

In football and in business, there are people who want to hurt those they don't like. There are three objectives for evading the blindside tactic:

1. Identify which candidates might possibly harm you and why.
2. Protect yourself from being hurt without notice.
3. Correct any damage received and prosecute the person inflicting the damage.

Why might someone want to hurt you? They might be unreasonable or self-centered and want to hurt you without good cause. They might believe your kindness conceals an ulterior motive. They might take advantage of your honesty to cheat you. They might be jealous of what you have accomplished. They might want to gain from taking over your project after they have defeated you.

Some are easy to identify, such as people assigned to oversee your project but who object to most of your proposals. Others are more difficult to identify, like people who feel you got a project or promotion they think should have gone to them. In most organizations and families, there are some who just don't like you. If you know who they are, be kind to them and encourage them to just let you do what you were assigned to do without interference.

In football, some quarterbacks are injured when their protection breaks down. It is always a surprise when the defense didn't help. This happened in our personal lives. We funded a facility inside the hospital to provide rooms where out-of-town families could stay while their loved one was hospitalized. The facility was named after us—our legacy.

After this facility had operated very successfully for twenty-five years, a new hospital president decided, on his own, to convert the facility for use by traveling nurses—to meet a current need, according to him. We were blindsided when, nine months later, a whistleblower inside the hospital sent us a copy of the plans to rebuild our facility. We felt like a quarterback who had been knocked out for lack of protection.

What conclusions can you draw from this story? First, you cannot trust anyone who puts their personal interest above someone else's. Second, when a blindside occurs you cannot count on anyone to tell you. Why? It's not their problem, or they don't want to be a whistleblower. Third, if you don't find out early that you have been blindsided, there may not be time to repair the damage.

In professional football, the player protecting the quarterback is carefully selected for his size and speed, is well-paid, practices daily, and has as his only goal the protection of the quarterback. That type of role does not exist in the business world.

To deal with blindsiders, you need people who can identify them, try and stop them from hurting you, and if they execute a plan to hurt you, to become a whistleblower and expose them. Who might these people be? Your colleagues who have your best interest at heart, your bosses who doesn't want unnecessary problems hurting their projects, and bystanders who come across a deliberate blindside who may or may not know you but do not want their employer harmed.

Another method is what auditors called the smell test—if something stinks, they bring it to your attention. The same test can be helpful to you as a project leader.

From an auditor's viewpoint, here are the tactics a project leader can use to protect against being blindsided:

- Realize in this world some people will hate you and want to hurt you.
- If you believe any of those people are involved in your project, or they have made it known they don't like what you're doing, try to compromise with them so they won't interfere with your work.
- Keep appraised of whatever smells bad to you and investigate.
- If someone is actively trying to hurt you, tell them to stop. This is not the time to be nice. If they continue, collect evidence and call in your management.
- If your project has been damaged, stop working until you have located and assess the damage, then develop a plan to fix it.

Remember, blindsiding may be okay in football, but in your personal, business, family, and social life, it can steal your enjoyment. We don't have to accept this as just part of doing business. With the right tactics, we can avoid or recover from blindsiding.

Work Both Ends Of The Clock
For many bosses, when you work is more important
than what you do at work.

It has always amazed me the criteria bosses use to evaluate their employees. Most companies provide their managers with a form they must use once a year to evaluate each employee, but they do not ask them to evaluate employees every day based on what they do.

Dr. W Edwards Deming, one of the great quality pioneers, in his "14 Points for Quality Management," recommended eliminating annual performance appraisals, because he said they are a major cause of employees' lack of motivation.

Some bosses take this advice and evaluate their subordinates on what they do, but still too many evaluate their subordinates on sticking to rules such as getting to work on time, leaving no earlier than closing time, and sticking to the time allotted for lunch. If your boss is a "follow the rules" boss, then follow the rules.

Bill, a supervisor for a medium-size company, meets with his superior Ann to discuss raises for his employees. At the moment, the discussion centers on two administrators.

Cindy is a very efficient worker who completes her tasks quickly and with few errors. She also points out problems to Bill so he can handle them before they become costly. Cindy volunteers to work overtime at the office or at home during the crunches. In short, Cindy is Bill's best worker.

Dudley is a plodding worker. He is not particularly accurate and turns out far less work than Cindy. Dudley absolutely refuses to work overtime anywhere. However, you can set your watch by him. He arrives three minutes before starting time, takes exactly one hour for lunch, never leaves before quitting time, and keeps busy all day.

Bill tells Ann, "I'd like to see Cindy get a good raise this time. She deserves it."

Ann says, "You know, Bill, I've noticed that Cindy has poor work habits. The other morning, I dropped by to check on your department four minutes after starting time, and Cindy wasn't at her desk. I've also noticed that from time to time she leaves a few minutes early. And to top it off, sometimes she stays playing on her phone in the lunchroom when she should be back at work."

Needless to say, Bill will find it difficult to get Cindy a good raise. Like many managers, Bill's superior doesn't understand what the workers do, so she rates their performance on the time clock rather than on results.

Ann continues, "Dudley is a real workhorse; he always gets to work on time, never goofs off on his lunch hour, and I've never known him to leave early. I know you want Dudley to get a good raise, and I'll see that he gets it. We need more workers like him."

Cindy does not get a good raise. Instead, she learns a lesson from Dudley—the Both Ends of the Clock Tactic.

If Cindy had recognized that that her raise depended on the judicious use of six minutes a day, she would make more money with less effort. The Both Ends of the Clock Tactic merely requires Cindy to arrive at work three minutes early, keep lunch to one hour, and to leave three minutes late at night. This tactic unequivocally depends upon the manager's belief that what happens between the starting and closing hours of work is far less important than starting early and stopping late.

Management textbooks extol competence and hard work as the characteristics upon which advancement and raises should be based. Don't believe it. In actual practice, advancement is more often related to two factors: first, strict adherence to company policies and procedures; and second, people factors.

Her is a checklist of the criteria under each of these factors:

Non-Technical Policies (strict adherence required)
- Starting work on time
- Taking a short lunch hour
- Leaving after closing time
- Never parking in the boss's parking spot
- Looking busy

Non-Technical People Factors
- Ability to get along
- Friendliness with those outside your department
- Getting customers to say a good word about you
- Having blood relations or in-laws in strategic positions
- Seniority
- Good looks, good health, suitable age
- Education

- Having the right spouse
- Engaging in highly visible and acceptable community activities
- Adhering to a fashionable religion
- Having illustrious relatives

Note: To use this checklist effectively, you must determine your boss's ranking of each criterion.

Any employee who is willing to apply the Both Ends of the Clock Tactic will find it a real help in getting raises and promotions.

The Alibi File
Whether you do something or nothing, you'd better
be prepared to defend your position.

When there are no problems during a project, everyone will be a hero. However, when problems occur everybody is looking for "who done it." The bigger the problem, the more intense the search.

In August 2023, when a fire in Maui destroyed more than 2,200 buildings and killed more than one hundred people, everybody stated they were innocent of starting the fire. Once downed powerlines were identified as the cause, the electric company started playing the "blame game," accusing the fire department of not being thorough enough in putting out the initial fire. Meanwhile, citizens still want punishment, and dozens of lawsuits have been filed.

If you are the bad guy, you deserve the punishment that goes with it. However, if you are innocent and charged, you had better be prepared to defend yourself—thus the necessity of an alibi file.

Let's see how an alibi file works.

Project Needed Soon is expected to have its share of problems that might significantly delay completion. A meeting is called for all the involved parties to make some decisions.

Each participant arrives with something different. Some come only with an open mind. Others carry agendas, scratch pads, or notebooks. Still others bring folders containing previous meeting minutes and correspondence relating to the project.

Sam Sharp, the project leader, has a dominant role in the meeting. He carries a bulging briefcase plus an armful of papers into the room. None of this is handout materials. It is Sam's alibi file. Sam has been around the organization for a number of years and has numerous battle scars from his involvement in other projects. He is quite familiar with overruns, missed budgets, and misappropriation of responsibility.

At this stage of the game, Sam's primary interest is not in the success of the project, not in meeting the target dates, the size of the staff, or meeting the real needs of the organization. Sam's main interest is protecting Sam. Thus, in the true spirit of "Protect Thine Arse" is born the alibi file.

Let's watch Sam use his alibi file.

Sam's boss opens the meeting, noting that Sam's reports did not discuss a missing segment, and thus there's a potential for missing the target completion date.

Decisions about the project are needed. There are two parts of the project: Part X and Part Y. It appears Part Y is on target; Sam's report contained no status on Part X.

The chair of the meeting says, "What happened to Part X, Sam?"

Sam scurries through his alibi file with great dexterity, extracting his notes on a conversation with Freddie Fallguy at the coffee machine eight months and three days ago. "Here," Sam says, "is a note of what Freddie said on August 13: 'Your task is primarily to produce Part Y of the project.' From this conversation, Boss, I assumed that my effort should be largely directed to Part Y, and that seemed to be his understanding about the project. As a matter of fact"—Sam deftly dips into his alibi file—"my memo for the record of October 20, which I have right here, shows that I called Freddie and told him the project would, at a minimum, include Part Y. He certainly knew I was focusing on Part Y, and that seemed to be his understanding of the project too."

As you can see, the alibi file is quite effective.

If you are placed in a situation where you are responsible for producing something, there is always the possibility that you may produce nothing. There may be many reasons for this. As Murphy so eloquently put it, "Whatever can go wrong will, and at the worst possible moment."

Or you may find that, as project leader, you have been assigned to a project doomed to certain failure. In such cases, the alibi file can be a strong ally.

How is an alibi file developed? An alibi file should be prepared for each project you are responsible for.

- Select a place to store your alibi file—this may be a folder, binder, or accordion file.
- Create an index that should include key decision points, parts of the project, meeting dates, names of key people or whatever you think might be needed.
- Each document should be dated, include the names of people involved, and have an index identifier for its subject matter.
- Small project, small alibi file; big project, big alibi file.
- Carry your alibi file with you to any meeting at which you may be asked to defend yourself. It is much more important to answer an inquiry at the time of the inquiry, rather than to stop the meeting and go to find it.

What are the advantages of having an alibi file?
- You have facts to defend yourself.
- If people know you are doing it, they may stay closer to the truth.

What are the disadvantages of an alibi file?
- It may hurt your career if it makes people scared of you.
- It will not help you get promoted.

The Information Avalanche
When your boss wants to meddle in your work,
send an avalanche of information.

In the day-to-day saga of modern management, the boss often gets in the way of progress. Management insecurities often show up in their insistence on frequent meetings and interim progress reports. Such meetings and reports only slow you down at critical points in your project. It's obvious that you need some way to keep your boss informed enough that she doesn't slow you down.

Randy is given the job of developing specifications for a new computer system, a job which calls for long hours of work to meet the demanding schedule. Randy uses every minute to his best advantage. He consults with many experts and documents every step. Randy is sure his thoroughgoing approach will please his boss.

However, from the boss's perspective, things don't look good at all. True, Randy seems busy, but he never seems to have time to talk about the project. His boss suspects that Randy's preoccupation with the task at hand is due to having fallen behind schedule. After all, his boss reasons, everybody knows that if you let someone do a job without supervision, he will slack off.

So like any good manager, the boss calls Randy on the carpet to berate him for falling behind schedule.

After listening to his boss's insults and innuendos about falling behind on the project, Randy pleads, "I have been working very hard. The project is even ahead of schedule, and I am very pleased with the way things are going."

"Randy," his boss says loudly, "If you had things under control, you would've reported to me about the project. As it is, I can't be sure we're going to meet the delivery date."

Randy thinks if he just works harder his boss will praise him. He works longer every day. He even comes in to work on Saturdays.

Then his boss storms into Randy's office, demanding that he "get moving on the project."

The next day Randy visits his friend Sam. After he explains the problem, Sam says, "What you have to do, Randy, is learn how to manage your manager."

"How do I manage my manager?" asks a bewildered Randy.

"There are lots of ways," Sam says, "but in this case the remedy is simple—you have to use a diversionary tactic to keep your boss off your back until the project is done. The tactic that will work here is creating a series of information avalanches."

"How do I do that?"

"Send your boss copies of all the worksheets you have done to date on the project, including notes from interviews, work papers, statistics, and checklists showing what you've done."

"What good will on that do?" Randy moans. "My boss hardly knows anything about computers or my project. I don't see what she'll learn from all that, or how it would keep her off my back."

"You've got a lot to learn. Managers like your boss become insecure when they think you haven't taken them into your confidence during the working phase of a project. They're convinced that employees won't work unless they're closed they supervised. Of course, your boss doesn't know enough about what you're doing to really supervise, so she wants reports. She wants to see quantities of work that will reassure her something is happening on the project."

"You're right, Sam! I can just see my boss going over the documents—she won't be able to make heads or tails of them, but I bet she will love them."

Sam's advice to Randy was to slide an avalanche of documents over to his boss periodically. This would overcome her "no watch no work" attitude.

Here are the simple rules of the Information Avalanche Tactic:
- Send your boss a copy of all outgoing correspondence. If she doesn't get a copy, she won't believe you sent it.
- Send your boss copies of incoming correspondence.
- Send your boss copies of worksheets, statistics, reports, and whatever else will keep her busy.
- When in doubt, send a memo. It's much better to send the boss too much than too little.

The best way to use the information avalanche is to keep a little information descending on your boss every day.

Show and Tell
The only purpose for a staff meeting is
to ensure that your boss thinks all is well.

In 4003 BC, a man called Hikiahn Staff organized a spear-making business. In just a few months, Hikiahn hired an employee to search for flints to be used as spearheads. Like most managers, Hikiahn Staff did not trust his employee, and wanted to meet with him regularly. These meetings were called Hikiahn Staff meetings. A couple of years later, the name was shortened to "staff meetings."

We have called these meetings between management and subordinates staff meetings ever since. The first staff meeting was held 6,027 years ago, and we should remember this for two reasons: first, it was the first staff meeting ever held and second, Hikiahn's employee was the first employee to dread staff meetings. He was the forerunner of all the poor employees who dread modern-day staff meetings.

Staff meetings may be the oldest form of corporate ritual. Certainly it is the most painful, followed shortly by being fired. Today's managers call staff meetings for many reasons. High on the list are first, getting you to do something you do not want to do, and second, telling you that management does not like what you have already done.

For example, at one sales meeting you're told your sales quota has been raised to lower your commission, and then at another, in front of the entire staff, you may be reprimanded for failing to meet your sales quota.

There are five basic types of staff meetings:

Managerial lecture. At this meeting, the manager does all the talking. He tells you what you did wrong, or demands you do things you do not want to do. The lecture design for two-year-olds. To be sure you didn't miss the point, he repeats it several times.

Show and tell. At this type of meeting, the manager assembles the troops and asks them, one by one, to show and tell what they've done since the last meeting (or what they will do until the next meeting). Experienced subordinates attend these meetings with a variety of PowerPoint slides, charts, and handouts. When nobody at the meeting can understand the slides, charts, and handouts, it's no problem, because managers love show and tell.

The critique. During this discouraging meeting, the boss asks various subordinates specific questions or has them explain the status of each project. When the workers finishes their explanations, the boss explains how they could've done better. These sessions could also be called hindsight meetings. Bosses love them because bosses always turn out to have 20/20 vision during these sessions.

The combination. These meetings are the most devastating of all staff meetings. This one begins with the traditional show and tell approach, then proceeds to the critique phase, and winds up with the grand finale management lecture. The aftereffects of this meeting are almost always the same: nausea, headache, and severe depression on the part of everybody but the one who called the meeting.

The ruin your Saturday meeting. Four of us reported to the same boss. All week we all looked very busy because if he saw us with our heads up or away from our desks, he would assign us more work. To "help" us, he said he would be available Saturday morning from 8 a.m. to noon so we could consult with him about anything and plan for the future. He said it was optional, but all except myself showed up, and I was punished by him for not coming in Saturday morning.

To the best of everybody's memory, the last good news to come out of a staff meeting was in 1901, when Henry Ford announced his workers' wages would be raised from $2.10 a day to $5 a day. Shortly after that, President Woodrow Wilson initiated the national income tax. That too, was announced at a staff meeting.

You probably already know how dreadful staff meetings are. Perhaps the only way they could be worse is to have meetings late on Friday afternoon. Knowing that staff meetings are inevitable, is there any way possible for someone to miss going to a staff meeting? The answer is yes. Make note of these staff meeting dodge tactics, because some day they will come in handy:

Judicious use of annual leave. Will Workman has ten days of annual vacation. He will use five of those in half-day increments on Friday afternoons. You guessed it—his boss's staff meetings are on Friday afternoons.

Tell the boss I'm sick. Penny Push's female complaints coincide with staff meetings. Since her boss is no gynecologist, what can he say? Anyone who is already out sick will not come back on staff meeting days, and anyone who feels the least bit sick will leave before the staff meeting starts.

Transportation problem ploy. Ken always has a flat tire at lunch on Friday.

Travel schedule dodge. This one really works. Randy schedules all his out of town travels to coincide with staff meetings.

My boss always had his staff meeting at three o'clock on Friday afternoons. He said he knew none of us would leave before five o'clock for the weekend, so having his meetings at that time would let us "start the weekend on a high note." Unless you wanted to use a meeting dodge tactic, you had to attend.

Since you must inevitably face that staff meetings are not optional, you must learn how to cope with them. The trauma of a staff meeting is proportional to its length, so your goal should be to leave in reasonably good health with your sanity intact. There are seven tactics for doing this:

Never argue with the manager. In group situations, the manager must appear to be the boss. Only in one-on-one situations can the boss change his mind and still save face.

Prearrange an early exit. This is easily accomplished through an emergency phone call or a visit from your secretary or a coworker who can say you're desperately needed to handle something you know your boss wants done.

Fantasize. By daydreaming of happy events or planning your next vacation, you'll be able to ignore the proceedings of the meeting. This worked for prisoners of war.

Write letters or documents. You have no friends at most meetings. Why not keep up your correspondence with those you love while you listen to those you don't like? I wrote the first version of this book during 138 staff meetings. Besides, your boss will be impressed. He'll think you're taking notes.

Don't participate. No matter what you say, it will only make the meeting longer.

Plan a pleasant event to follow the meeting. Knowing that a Danish and hot coffee are waiting for you right after the meeting can help.

Pray for the end of all unpleasantness in the world. Surely that will include all staff meetings.

Never accept that all your happiness will never be the same after a staff meeting, because as long as you know how to dodge staff meetings and the seven ways of enduring staff meetings, there will be a light at the end of each staff meeting.

The Golden Handcuffs
Benefits are chains designed to keep you in place.

Businesses add benefits to a job to entice people to work for them. For employees, benefits are nontaxable income. Those looking for a job consider not only the salary but the benefits when deciding whether or not to take a job. Some benefits are more important than salary. Employees see benefits as an entitlement, not a component of salary.

Employers consider benefits as part of salary, and many companies quantify benefits so employees know how much their benefits are worth. In many companies, the cost of benefits is approximately to 30 percent to 50 percent of an employee's salary.

When an employee is considering a new job, however, many do take into account the value of benefits. A good medical plan may be more valuable to a worker than the salary. To an employer, the term *golden handcuffs* means if the benefit is good enough it will chain an employee to their job, so they won't leave the company.

If you love freedom, you must pay attention to benefit plans. They are used to lure you into staying with your employer. If you stay with a company long enough to let your benefits mature, you have been lured into the company trap, and the door to leave has been slammed shut on you. The organization knows it's gotcha, and you know it's gotcha. From that moment on, you can either be in big trouble, or be happy as a lark, depending on whether you really like your job.

Once you know the golden handcuffs theory, you begin to wonder who benefits the most from your benefits plan. Examine the plan closely, because not all benefits are obvious.

The number one benefits a company holds out are comfort and security. Many of us are just like our manager. We hate change. We want our job to be comfortable—wearing our old clothes, at our old desk, in our old chairs—doing our old job. If we feel comfortable and secure, we are likely to remain with the company—even if we dislike our job.

The second benefits a company offers are permanency, friends, and familiarity. The very thought of packing up and leaving can outweigh many personal dislikes.

Other major fringe benefits include vacations, pension plans, sickness benefits, a company store or discount, social events, sports leagues, and so on. All of these can be measured in dollars and cents—as our bosses have pointed out to us many times. And, as is the case with other benefits, the longer we stay with our organization, the more valuable they become.

As we grow older, the value of our benefit package increases, as our marketability to other organizations deceases. Equal opportunity notwithstanding, most companies believe that people over forty are not desirable as new employees. The fact is that most managers believe anyone over forty that can break the golden handcuffs is not dependable or loyal—such people are looking for work they *enjoy*, and what manager wants employees like that?

When we started a small business, we were surprised by what candidates wanted to know. They would ask if they got fifteen-minute breaks morning and afternoon, how many days of vacation, sick time and holidays they would get, and about our health insurance and retirement benefits. Only a few asked questions about the tasks they would be assigned.

When we calculated our cost for their benefits, which averaged 30 percent or more of their salary, and told each employee the dollar value of their benefits, it meant nothing to them; they assumed they were entitled to it. For example, if they would further their education we would fully pay their school tuition, so the most they would pay was for books, plus using their time after work for learning. Very few ever wanted this benefit, because they had to do something to get it. Also, instead of giving a year-end bonus, we offered to put 150 percent of their bonus into a 401(k) plan. No employee wanted that gift; they wanted the smaller amount of money immediately. At year end, some of our employees said we had cheated them by withholding federal tax and social security deductions from their salary.

Why would an employee want to leave their employer? There are many reasons most commonly they don't like their job, or want to do something different or more meaningful to them. In other cases they are uncomfortable with the organization or the boss is a micromanager. Some leave because they are not advancing in job and salary as rapidly as they feel they should. Some leave for personal reasons—to move nearer to family, relocate to a different climate, change their profession, or start a business.

How can you break the chains that bind you? Only through determination, good planning, and a strong desire to be free.

You may find the very benefits that tie you to your employer can be your path out of the golden handcuffs. For example, you may have built up enough equity in your retirement plan to carry you for a year without a salary, giving you time for you to move where you want to live and find a new job. Sometimes a company needing to reduce staff will give you a lot money if you will retire early. That's freedom now.

Another way to seek freedom is to take a piece of paper, and on one side list the things you want out of life and your job, and on the other side of the page list your current life style and job conditions. Here is a typical list:

WHAT I WANT	WHAT I HAVE
I would like to travel	I never leave home or office
I would like a warm climate	I am cold half the year
I would like to be my own boss	I am a slave to my boss
I wish I could be more creative	I do repetitive jobs all the time
I want enough money to live well	I have enough money to live well
I want a nice home	I have a nice home

After fifteen years at Kodak, in my mid-forties, I did this exercise, and here are my results: I wanted to live in a warm climate—I lived in Rochester, New York, a frigid climate. I had more than enough money to have a good life—I could take a 25 percent cut in salary and still be happy. I did not want a micromanager as my boss—I had a micromanager for a boss. I wanted a nice home—If I sold my house, I could buy a nice home in a warmer climate. I wanted a job that was innovative and creative—I no longer had a creative and innovative job. Eventually I wanted my own business—I had an idea for a business, but did not feel ready to start one. I wanted to be a college professor—I was already a part-time college professor.

My analysis told me I was a candidate for seeking a new location and a new job. I looked around and found an innovative job as the research director for the Institute of Internal Auditors in Orlando, Florida. The perfect job for me. I applied and got it, and lived happily ever after.

The Pocket Veto
A pocket veto is another way of rejecting ideas
by saying "I'll think about it."

One of the most powerful of all management tools is the pocket veto. It is used by all levels of management right up to the president of the United States. This technique is used by managers to avoid that most dreaded act—making a decision.

As a subordinate, you must not forget that decisions terrify managers because any decision can be wrong. Managers never want to be wrong.

The pocket veto is a technique used to avoid making decisions. This accounts for its popularity. The method is simple. The manager just puts the request for a decision in a "pocket" and leaves it there until the subordinate forgets about it and gives up. Managers have several names for these pockets: in basket, tickler file, suspense file, and bottom drawer.

Here are the simple steps of a pocket veto:
1. The subordinate requests a manager makes a decision on their suggestion.
2. The manager asks the subordinate to put the suggestion in writing. (This dodge alone is estimated to eliminate three out of five decisions.)
3. The subordinate give the a manager a write-up, complete with recommendations.

4. The manager places the write up in a pocket, and that's that is the last anyone ever hears of it.

Penny Push thought that giving employees five sick days a year was a poor use of days off, because few employees got sick, so they called in "sick" to do personal tasks, like going out on the first day of hunting season. To do this they had to lie.

Penny suggested to her boss, "Let's eliminate sick days, give employees five more days of vacation, and if they do get sick, that time can be taken from their vacation days."

He said, "Very interesting, Penny. I'll need to think about it." Then he added, "Oh by the way, would you write up your suggestion with the rationale and give it to me?"

Penny thought she had explained her suggestion well enough, but if her boss wanted it in writing she must be making progress. Little did she know that once her memo was in a pocket veto it would take an act of Congress to get it out.

Penny needed to know two things about the pocket veto: First, it is extremely powerful and it is used everywhere. Second, the manager usually tips his hand as to whether or not your idea has already been vetoed by using statements like these:

- I'll need to think about it
- I'll get to it as soon as possible
- I'll have to discuss it with my boss
- That is a very interesting idea.

The other thing you need to know about the pocket veto is how to unpocket your suggestion. Unpocketing maneuvers are accepted by management if they are not practiced too often. While unpocketing will not always get the results you want, in most cases it will force a decision.

Here are five successful unpocketing tactics listed in order of their known success rate, with the best first:

Carbon Copy: When you send your suggestion to your boss send a copy to his boss or someone with a vested interest in your idea.

Public Issue: At a departmental staff meeting, you can raise your question to your manager in front of all his subordinates. It helps if you can get support from your coworkers prior to the meeting. Pocket vetoes are more difficult for managers to pull off when two or more subordinates are involved.

Creeping Commitment: Big decisions are traumatic for managers. If you believe your idea has been pocket vetoed because the idea was too big a decision for your boss to make, go back with a smaller version of your idea, or just a part of your idea. For example, with Penny's sick day idea, she could ask to change three sick days to vacation instead of five. Small changes are much easier to approve than large ones.

Suggestion Box: Many large organizations have a suggestion box. If you put your suggestion in the box, it must be answered. If accepted, you have won. However, only about 10 percent of suggestions put in the box are excepted. If rejected, they must tell you the reason. The reason for rejection will give you ammunition for the next battle if you plan to try again later.

Business is a game of pocketing and unpocketing vetoes. Since managers always fights savagely for the status quo, any attempt to change things will stand a good chance of being pocket vetoed. Be alert. Learn how to remove your suggestion from your superiors' pockets. That may be pickpocketing, but it's profitable. Remember, when your idea's been stuck in a pocket, use these tactics to get it on docket.

Fossilization Theory
A fossilized person is one who has joined
the league of active retired.

A scientific definition of a fossil is the remains of animal life from some previous age.

A business definition of a fossil is a person with fixed ideas and no remaining creative capabilities. They continually talk about the "good old days." A fossilized brain is like a tape recording—the only words you can get from it are the words already on the tape.

Why should good employees be concerned about fossils at work? Two reasons: first, they cannot contribute anything creative to a workplace, and second, they will disrupt discussions of all new ideas, because they believe any worthwhile idea has already been invented.

You need to identify the fossils in your workplace and keep them away from almost anything you are doing.

People can fossilize at any age. For them, it is synonymous with retirement. Some organizations call fossils the "active retired," meaning they contribute very little, but as long as they work for the company, they will get paid.

One of the youngest fossils in history was Dee Endd, who joined the company at age twenty-two, became a fossil at twenty-seven, and is still working there at forty-seven. What happened to Dee between when she was hired after graduating magna cum laude from a major Ivy League business school and when she fossilized?

During her first three years, she spent two months in each of eighteen different departments, doing busy work while learning how the company operated. Dee lived in anticipation of her first real assignment, as an assistant to the administrative assistant of the accounting department.

During orientation, she learned the importance of getting to work on time, keeping her breaks no longer than allowed, keeping detailed records of her job duties, performing little jobs for the boss, and arriving to staff meetings on time.

The lack of any real responsibilities left her discouraged. She strongly disagreed with her boss about not incorporating new technologies, and lost. A special assignment was given to her, but when it failed, she got the blame. She finally decided she had no future at her company. On her twenty-seventh birthday she became a fossil and has been considered a model employee ever after. Since becoming a fossil, she has not done anything wrong; she also has not done anything creative.

If you want to succeed in business, you must avoid becoming a fossil for two reasons. First, as a fossil you will no longer enjoy your job. Second, if you succeed at work long enough to get management's respect, you can achieve a good position, and have fossils working for you. Is it worth having fossils working for you? Yes, most of the time. Fossils cause no problems. They never stab you in the back. They don't want your job or the credit for your work. On the other hand, you need to learn how to recognize fossils and how to use them.

How can you recognize a fossil? By their blind adherence to company policies and procedures. Fossils wear them as a badge of honor. Any deviation requires a fossil to accept responsibility, which is out of the question. Also, they love the status quo; any kind of change makes them nervous.

How can you get a fossil to actually do work? Give them repetitive, routine tasks. They do those jobs well. Ask them to advise you on company policies and procedures, and assign them tasks that require an extensive knowledge of those policies and procedures. Just don't ask them to do anything creative or innovative. It isn't in them.

How do you motivate fossils? Their major enjoyment in life is telling employees and customers what cannot be done because it would violate company policy. Given such a job, they will be content until actual retirement twenty or more years in the future. I knew an employee whose doctor recommended an optional operation; the employee waited to have it done until he was asked to do something he did not want to do.

Are there many fossils out there in the business world? There are indeed. About seven of every ten employees over thirty years of age are fossilized to some degree. In his book *Creativity: Flow and the Psychology of Discovery and Invention*, psychology professor Mihaly Csikszentmihalyi notes that "a person whose thinking is fluent, flexible, and original is more likely to come up with novel ideas." Unfortunately, these are qualities the fossilized person lacks. So try to draw a few creative ideas from your colleagues before they fossilize. The creative professionals Csikszentmihalyi surveyed "often claimed to have had only two or three good ideas in their entire career, but each idea was so generative that it kept them busy for a lifetime."

Now you know how to keep from becoming a fossil. You aren't one, you know, or you wouldn't be reading this book. But keep checking. If you find signs of fossilization, take steps to stop the trend. If necessary, kick off the traces and infuse new life into the old you. If you haven't caught the disease of fossilization, there is still time to change jobs and find a challenge. Whatever you do, don't become an old fossil.

CHAPTER EIGHT

MMTs for Obtaining Manager Approval

Approvals are one of the great curses in life;
I now believe I cannot die without approval.

ALMOST ALL ORGANIZATIONS ARE hierarchical, meaning the CEO is at the top of the organization and in charge of everything. As some say, The Buck Stops Here. Below the CEO there may be many downward levels of authority, until it stops with you. You are given some authority in your job description, and your boss can give or reject approval for almost everything else you may be responsible to do. For example, to spent $20,000 for new computers, you may need approval from a level above your boss.

There are many means of issuing approvals, including orally, in writing, or via pre-approval for some emergencies.

Getting most approvals is easy, but in some cases you may be challenged for any number of reasons:

- The person authorized to grant the approval is not available.
- The approving party wants more time to study the request
- The approving party is too busy to study your request.
- The approving party wants you to do something for them before they grant approval.

Not getting the approval when it's needed make cause you to miss your deadline, in which case you need to discuss with your boss how to handle the delay.

If you judge an action to be necessary for the company's success but choose not to request approval, you're risking the wrath of management.

The president of a hospital wanted to finish a project that was already 95 percent done, and he could not get funds approved for completion. He chose to move the needed amount from another account and completed the project. For that he was fired.

Another manager wanted to close a department and use the space for another purpose. He developed the plans, but before he could begin work, a whistleblower exposed his intentions. Management stopped his project and forced him to go through the formal approval process.

In other words, taking the bull by the horns—or asking forgiveness rather than permission—isn't always praised even when it's what is right for the organization.

Circumventing approval is a personal choice; it is risky. How managers react can vary from ignoring what you did, to praising you, or inflicting punishment. See Chapter Nine for MMTs to help overcome roadblocks.

The tactics in this chapter are just good business practices designed to make it easy for your managers to *want* to give you approval.

The Creeping Commitment Tactic
It is easier to get many small decisions than one big decision.

You complete a project on time, so you ask your manager if you can take your ten employees to McDonald's for lunch. Total cost: $60. Approved.

Later, you ask if you all could go to a deli instead: it's only $40 more. Approved.

Oops, some employees don't have cars. Can you rent a van to take everyone to lunch? It's only $75. Approved.

While we're at it, can we give each employee a $25 gift card for a job well done? Approved.

Now, instead of the original $60, the total value of team rewards is now $425.

At each decision point, the manager only had to approve a small amount, not the total. Creeping commitment is a great tactic if you're asking, but not so great when you are paying the bill.

Creeping commitment can be voluntary or involuntary. If you know this tactic, you can make it work for you. You can get a large decision made by starting with a small decision. If you see a creeping commitment coming, you can cancel the initial request or limit the total cost of the project.

Here is an example of a runaway commitment. Mr. Marvelous is planning a summer vacation at the beach for his family, and has a budget to pay for it. The whole family is looking forward to this vacation, including Mrs. Marvelous. However, she also wants to update her living room. She opts to use the Creeping Commitment Tactic to pay for it.

Mrs. Marvelous knows she can probably not get the money without impacting their family vacation, so she only asks to replace one threadbare velvet chair. A local store has a pretty yellow chair for only $399, so she buys it and has it delivered. It looks great in her living room; however, she thinks it clashes with the flowered purple wallpaper.

The next day she scans the internet and finds someone who can remove the wallpaper for $350. Another person can paint the walls for $400, using a beige color that gives just the right emphasis for the yellow chair.

Guess what, she next buys a new sofa ($600), coffee table ($400), and a new lamp ($250). What happened? By making six small decisions they thought they could afford, they ended up with a new living room at a cost of $2,399. As a result, they could no longer afford their summer vacation.

Mrs. Marvelous can't believe they had to give up their summer vacation, when all she did was buy one chair!

No, Mrs. Marvelous, you are a victim of creeping commitment.

Even having children is a creeping commitment. If you knew it would cost $400,000 to raise a child for eighteen years, you might approach sex more cautiously. It is the uncounted, the unforeseen, that enables you to make small decisions too quickly.

Making creeping commitment work for you is a three-phase process.

Phase One is to alert your boss to a problem. For example, employees are going home for lunch, or eating at their desk. If they go home, they do not get back to work on time; if they eat at their desk, some foods smell and others cause stains. Until the boss recognizes there is a problem, you can go no further.

Phase Two begins when the boss does recognize the problem. She will be look for a solution, so now you volunteer to undertake that study. Wait some time before concluding Phase Two, which is proposing a solution after studying the problem. Approving the study is a small decision, made without knowing how much the solution will cost, but the commitment to spend has started. Your lunch break study may show that the solution would be to make a space where employees can eat. This would eliminate food odors, soiled desks, and enable a firm policy to be made regarding the time allotted for lunch. The study to solve a problem does not mention costs.

Phase Three begins when the boss gives permission to implement the solution. You might rework a storeroom to put in a table where employees can eat. You do this knowing whoever runs the storeroom will want that space back. Once the employees are happy with a dedicated lunchroom and morale and production are up, and you are told you must vacate the storeroom, you propose what you wanted before you told the boss there was a problem: a full lunchroom with a kitchen at a cost of $75,000. The boss is committed, so the lunchroom is built.

It takes a very creative subordinate to get a manager to make the first small decision that will creep up to a point where a large decision must be made. The creeping commitment tactic works because big decisions are hard to make, and very painful for managers. Using creeping commitment makes life easier for both you and your manager, and helps your company at the same time.

The PDCA Process
If you fail to plan, plan to fail.

Most people, when they acquire a product that needs to be assembled, just look at the picture on the box and immediately begin assembling the product. They don't read the instructions or verify that the box actually contains all the needed parts. There is even a saying to support this: "If all else fails, read the instructions."

Many people believe planning is a waste of time, but in fact insufficient planning is almost always a costly mistake.

At the end of World War II, general Douglas MacArthur was appointed to oversee the reconstruction of Japan. As Japanese manufacturing plants resumed operations, their products came out very poor. In the U.S. market, Japanese products were considered close to junk, often requiring extensive repairs.

One of the most respected pioneers of quality control was Dr. W. Edwards Deming. General MacArthur invited Dr. Deming to visit Japan with the goal of improving the quality of Japanese products. He did, and within a few years Japanese products were considered some of the best in the world. That reputation continues even to the present. How did he do it?

First, he developed his "14 Principles of Quality Management." (I recommend looking them up; you can find them at the website of the American Society for Quality: asq.org.) Second, he used his four-step process for producing quality products. These four steps are Plan Do Check Act, known as PDCA.

Here's how to employ the PDCA Process:

1. Before you start a project, develop an extensive **Plan** to ensure you will be successful.

2. As you **Do** the work of the project, use the specifications in your plan

3. **Check** the work (a process commonly called quality control) to assure that the product you've built meets the product specifications and will be acceptable to the customer or user.

4. If the product does not pass its Check, you must **Act** to correct any faults or defects and make changes to the process to prevent such faults in the future.

Now you know the basics of how to build a quality product. If this is a new topic for you, consider taking a course or reading a book on planning. These are skills that will benefit you throughout your career, because planning is the most important step toward success. There are two reasons this is true: economics and time.

Economics is a cost issue. Phillip Crosby, the author of *Quality is Free*, promoted a concept called Cost of Quality. There are three components to calculating the cost of building a defect free-product:

1. **The cost to build** a product or provide a service includes both planning and execution (Deming's P and D).

2. **The cost of quality control**, or assuring that the completed product or service meets specifications (C).

3. **The cost to fix** the product if it doesn't meet the specifications, usually called repair cost (A).

If you buy a child's toy unassembled, but when you open the box there's a part missing, you now have a cost to fix. You have to contact the manufacturer and request the missing part. The manufacturer has to assign someone to find the part and ship it to you. Then you spent time waiting for the part to arrive before you can try again to assemble your child's toy. Often the cost to fix is greater than the combined costs of building and quality control.

What is a quality product? First, it means we have assured that the product built or service performed was done according to specifications. This type of quality is called **quality in fact**. Second, we have **quality in perception**, meaning the consumer of the product or service is satisfied with what they received.

If you ask a hair stylist to leave your hair long and they cut it short, they lack quality in fact; they didn't meet your specification.

If you try a new nail polish and it works fine but you don't like how it looks, you have a lack of quality in perception.

Decades ago, the Ford Motor Company built what they thought was the car of the future. It was called the Edsel. As presented to the public, the Edsel met Ford's specifications. The problem was that car buyers did not like the Edsel, and soon it was no longer manufactured.

When a major aircraft manufacturer built a certain aircraft, the delivered airplane met their specifications. However, pilots could not fly the plane safely due to a faulty flight control system. The cost to fix this aircraft was tens of billions of dollars.

What could Ford or the aircraft manufacturer have done to avoid their products' failure? Most manufacturers today use focus groups, which comprise potential users of the product or service to determine whether they want and would buy the product.

Now that you know the basics about quality, quality management, the cost of quality, and the value of planning, how do you use that information to manage successfully?

First, understand that effective planning is a costly and time-consuming part of manufacturing a product or delivering a service.

However, if your manager wants you to reduce planning and start building right away, don't let that happen. If you have ever watched a contractor build a home or an office building, you realize how long it takes to build a solid foundation versus the time needed to build the rest of the project. If you have ever traveled to Pisa, Italy, and viewed the Leaning Tower, you can appreciate the importance of a good foundation. To manage management, you need to make project leaders aware that extensive planning is necessary for success. Using the cost of quality process to analyze what happened on an unsuccessful project may help you teach this planning lesson.

Second, if you're building a product or providing a service, never shortcut planning even when your management wants you to stop planning and start building. One important lesson I learned from a salesperson was that, prior to making a sales call to offer a new product for a customer to buy, you must spend much more time planning and rehearsing for the meeting than will be spent at the meeting itself. By doing this kind of planning, every salesperson in that ompany was prepared to answer any question a customer might have, then offer a solution to address that concern. By offering solutions for any concern that might cause the customer not to buy the product, they usually made the sale.

When you go to an auto dealership, you know how much you can spend, and the dealer knows how much they can lower the price so you will buy the car you want. Both parties can then play the game known as *negotiation*. Usually, the one who has done a better job of planning wins the game.

The Rathole Theory
If you run out of funds—ignore all past costs,
and start again.

A rathole is a bottomless pit. Sometimes you must ignore all the past costs of your project when making a decision to spend more on it.

If you buy a car for $10,000, and after three years the engine needs repairs costing $2,000, you can save $8,000 by fixing your current car instead of buying another car for $10,000. That gives you a great return on the repair investment. Is this good accounting? Probably not, but most people believe it. This is why the Rathole Theory can work for you.

The Rathole Theory is the cornerstone of corporate finance, government spending, and family budgeting. Yet few know it by name. Great economists such as Adam Smith and John Maynard Keynes developed theories of economics upon which government leaders debate. Great centers of learning such as the University of Pennsylvania have prepared elaborate models on spending. The term they use is *sunk costs*. But when you've said *rathole*, you've said it all.

To see how the Rathole Theory works, let's consider a typical domestic rathole—your TV set. Let's say your current set cost $600 three years ago, and it is paid for. With any luck, your TV set will last the first three years without any problems. At the end of three years, you have a choice. Buy a new TV set, or start repairing the old set. One night during your favorite TV show, the set goes blank. The repair tech, after a $50 call to your home, estimates it will cost $90 to fix. What should you do? The typical homeowner will reason that a new set now costs $750, and it will only cost $90 to fix this one, so I'll save money if I just spend the $90. You do that, and the set comes to life again. With a sigh of relief and a scotch in your hand, you settle back for another three years of TV.

Two months later, the TV is on the fritz again. This time your smiling technician estimates that for $100, they can make your TV as good as new. The rathole theory says ignore the previous expenditure and compare the cost of a new set at $750, against the cost of repairing the old set for $100. In most people's minds, what is spent is "down the rathole," and therefore, not considered.

Never mind what you'll do the next time the TV is on the blink. Just say, "rathole."

How does this tactic work in business? And how can you use it to get what you want? Let's see how Denny Dart uses it. Denny frequently clashes with his boss about buying a new accounting software system.

Denny's boss is trying to hold the line on spending. He said at the last staff meeting, "From now on all new projects must show a positive return on investment." The boss made that announcement just prior to Denny submitting a proposal for the new accounting system.

The system Denny recommends would cost $50,000 and would save his staff a lot of time—but not $50,000 worth. He figures the reduction in overtime and tech support will only be worth about $40,000 a year, so it would take more than a year to recoup the cost of the new system.

To get his project approved, Denny knew he needed the rathole theory. Through some innovative accounting, Denny reduces the cost of the project to $35,000. He uses two phases of the tactic. Phase One is to propose a $35,000 expenditure that will save the company $40,000, making for a $5,000 return on investment.

The project is approved.

Phase Two comes into play when, after $35,000 is already spent, more money is needed to finish the project. Denny Dart goes in prepared like a con man moving cups around so you can't tell which cup the pea is under.

Denny tells his boss the sad story of how this and that caused him to run out of money before the project was complete. Then he requests another $15,000 to complete the project. Otherwise they will have wasted $35,000.

Nice move, Denny, but how will his boss look at it?

The boss approves the additional expenditure, since spending another $15,000 to finish is less costly than losing $35,000 with nothing to show for it. The boss thinks Denny should be promoted for saving the project. Clearly the boss doesn't know which cup the pea is under.

Pray, dear reader, how do you appraise the performance of Denny Dart? Did he get what he wanted? Is he a genius? Should he be promoted or fired? Knowing what I know about management, I bet he gets promoted, because management thinks about the future, not the past. The old rathole theory seldom fails. Out of sight, out of mind.

This is a fun story to read, and it has a lot of truth in it. However, I don't suggest using a scam to get what you want. However, the rathole theory may help when you find yourself failing to meet your budget and schedule. If a lot of time and money has been invested in a project, often it truly is better to invest more to rescue the project than to cut losses and bail.

Variations of this tactic are used all the time. I wanted to get a new electric toothbrush—it seemed expensive, but I could afford it. So I bought it, but I failed to realize I had fallen into a rathole. The manufacturer had changed the design, so my old heads didn't fit in the new handle. They also raised the cost of the replacement heads.

Awareness of this tactic can help you avoid falling into a rathole yourself.

The Walking Encyclopedia Tactic
Cite a figure, make it stick; lots of stats will turn the trick.

Statistics can be your best friend for getting approval to do what you want. However, the implementation of this tactic requires nurturing over time.

We read statistics every day in papers, magazines, social media, and on cable news. We believe these statistics because they are numerical, which tells us someone did a lot of work to gather them. The numbers we tend to doubt are round numbers, for example, there is a 40 percent chance of rain today—an educated guess.

The questions we need to ask are: Who conducted the study that produced the statistics? Are they recognized as reliable? Who participated in the study? How big was the sample size? How was the sample selected? And more.

The scary part is how many decisions we make based on unreliable statistics. What we do know is that those who know statistics have an advantage in the workplace over those who lack statistics to support their positions.

Be one of those people who have statistics to support their position.

One of my best friends owned a market research firm. Clients would ask him to do a study on some issue or product, and produce statistics they could use in their marketing. This researcher taught me the criteria for good reliable statistics. They are statistics drawn from an independent group with a size of more than thirty, using questions that are not biased, and presented in a statically correct way.

I asked him, "How can the reader of a statistic know that the numbers generated were based on sound statistical theory?"

"They can't. In fact, if a client wants a specific conclusion, I can develop a data collection process to produce the exact result the client wants."

That shattered my opinion of the validity of the statistics presented in marketing material.

What did I learn from my friend, a well-known market researcher, is that you can use statistics to prove anything, and that most who read the statistics don't know and don't care how they were developed.

Scientific management is in, and seat-of-the-pants management is out. Modern managers use game theory, regression analysis, data analytics, and other scientific methods to reach decisions. However, while most managers believe in using scientific methods for decision making, many managers still rely on intuition and gut feelings. When these managers are presented with an impressive array of statistics when they are about to make decisions, they cannot interpret the statistics. Unfortunately, many of these same mangers understand very little about the data at their disposal.

For these reasons, the Walking Encyclopedia Tactic is very effective. This tactic posits that given the blind acceptance of "scientific management principles," statistics are irrefutable. Since this is so, you must present management with enough statistics to convince them you know what you are doing. Just as one more straw added to a capacity load will break the camel's back, so just one more statistic added to an "irrefutable" statistical argument will break down the resistance of a recalcitrant manager.

To illustrate the point, let's say you are invited to be an observer during the meeting of mid-level managers. They are meeting to decide on whether to computerize a certain segment of their operations. Tom Tough is assigned to do the feasibility study. Tom has one of the prime requisites to make this presentation—confidence. Management likes that. And nothing bolsters confidence better than "facts." Tom knows this, so he is a veritable walking encyclopedia.

To sell the idea of a new accounts receivable system, Tom begins by citing statistics. "Studies have shown it takes an average clerk seven and a half minutes to look up information on nonstandard requests. Applying the same methods of study to our unique situation, we find that our clerks spend six percent more time than the industry average. We also find that 2.1 invoices out of 40 must be rewritten because certain data are lacking when the invoice is first prepared. Based on these and other statistics—such as time spent correcting errors, time lost because of improper work flow, and the like—we will be able to remain at current staff levels for the next five years. This is based on statistics which show that the new system will be 13 percent more efficient in clerical entries, reduce errors 14.3 percent, and increase productivity by a whopping 16.3 percent. Based on an 8 percent increase in the cost of living, and the possibility of a 20 percent increase in the cost of benefits, we should realize a 17.5 percent return on investment."

By now, the eyes of all the managers present are wide open. This all sounds great to them.

And no wonder—Tom presents each statistic authoritatively and boldly. Keep in mind that while they may ask an occasional question, they really know very little about the technical trivia Tom triumphantly touts.

The Walking Encyclopedia Tactic requires that some of the statistics be factual. But what makes the tactic work is the abundance of commonly collected statistics that surround and gain credence from the valid statistics. The truth is, many of Tom's technical interpretations are very easy to find, and are just as impressive as the real thing.

When I ran the Quality Assurance Institute, I read about thirty-five documents a month, including many free publications about our industry, business letters and journals, conference presentations, and information from friends and colleagues, and across all of these, I never asked how authoritative the statistics were. I catalogued the statistics I got from these sources, and then used them in articles I wrote, in presentations, and for answering business colleagues when they wanted statistics. For example, many sources give annual salary by profession, which I used to answer many questions about the salary of quality assurance professionals.

How do you become a walking encyclopedia?

First, start collecting data. Begin as a daily part of your life to record statistics given to you by colleagues and when you see statistics quoted in articles relevant to your work. Use an old-school note-taking system like index cards, or store them digitally in a note-taking app.

Then, as appropriate, deploy your statistics among colleagues and at meetings. You'll be surprised that people rarely question statistics. Occasionally, someone may ask where you got a statistic. Answer by giving the source if you know it, otherwise just say you got it from a colleague.

Second, use one or two statistics in your official business meetings or reports; your confidence using statistics will improve. Then fill your meetings, proposals, and reports with numerous statistics. The more accurate your information, the more it will deter most people from to objecting to your proposals.

The Top Grape Tactic
Build a better rumor, and management will
beat a path to your door.

The Top Grape is the unofficial city editor of the most efficient means of communication known to man—the company grapevine. Gossip (sometimes called scuttlebutt, rumor, or leak), is the life-blood of communication in most organizations. Usually the source is unknown, as is the gossip's truth or falsity. Usually it doesn't matter. The grapevine is the means of transmitting gossip, and if the gossip is good, the grapevine works overtime to spread the juicy news within minutes. What most people don't know about gossip is that it is used both by management—to test the waters on something they are not sure how workers might react to—and by workers—to build support for something they want to happen.

Sam A. Stute and three fellow workers are at their coffee machine for their mid-morning break. They listen as Sam says, "Looks like the boss is looking for a replacement for Will Workman, because Will's heath is going downhill." He continues, "Swann Songue is the obvious replacement; he's been here thirty-one years, but his age is against him. Randy Rightman would be a good choice, but I think Penny Push will get the job."

"Why Penny Push?" Sam's friends ask.

"She's just as qualified as Randy," Sam said, "and our company lags behind others in our field in promoting women. So they kind of have to give it to her."

Sam's friends depart and begin spreading the rumor that Penny Push will get Will Workman's job.

Why do these three people have such confidence in Sam? Because he is the oracle of knowledge in their company—the Top Grape. If it has happened, might happen, or should happen, Sam knows and tells all.

In small organizations, only one top grape is needed. In large organizations, there may be several. In addition, there are people in the organization who know a secret and want to spread it to others. The medium grapes are sometimes called whistleblowers.

One interesting thing about the grapevine is that it permeates every level of the organization. No one is excluded from the vine's communication, and no one wants to be excluded. No message is too insignificant for the ears of the janitor, the CEO, or anyone in between. The top grape is appointed to their position, they have no job description, and they are not compensated for the time they spend working the grapevine. However, it is a highly coveted, important and honored position. The top grape and all the lesser grapes have several important responsibilities:

- Remember and pass along all gossip, rumors, stories, and even an occasional fact.
- Be available to talk about the latest happening at any time, in any place, and to anybody.
- Create useful and believable rumors during slack periods.
- Put rumors into historical perspective, thus making them more reliable.

To become a top grape, one must want the position and must have years of experience in the organization, along with an appearance of wide-eyed righteousness and honesty.

The unwritten job description includes: regular access to those in management positions; an overwhelming desire to speculate on what will happen; a reasonable degree of accuracy; bionic eyes, including the ability to read upside down while talking to people at their desk; the ability to enrich rumors and fill in the missing data; and, if possible, access to the boss's secretary, which will substantially improve your batting average. The top gape should have the ability to put up trial balloons to get management's reaction to top grape introduced rumors to see if they catch management's fancy.

Did Penny Push get Will Workman's job? Yes, and she used the top grape tactic to get it.

She knew Will Workman had a health problem, and that he missed twenty-two days of work this year. She got this information from Wendy Watch, who had to fill in for Will when he was out.

Knowing Sam was the top grape, Penny told him about Will's absences. Sam used that to create a rumor for management about Will wanting to retire.

When Wendy Watch read an article containing industry statistics about promotions for women and people of color and calculated that their company was behind on this metric, Penny shared that information with Sam, who passed it on to both management and staff members. This rumor put pressure on management, and Penny got the job.

Penny's intelligent use of the top grape theory worked for her, and it can work for you.

A final illustration will show the usefulness of the top grape theory in getting decisions made on a timely basis.

A snowstorm begins as workers arrive at the office. By noon, the parking lot is blanked by six inches of snow. A little before noon, Sam sees a problem, because by five o'clock, traffic will be snarled all over town, so employees could be involved in accidents, which could affect work schedules. As usual, upper management is not managing.

A lower manager tells Sam she had heard that the company might close at three o'clock, because she believes the workers may be disgruntled if the executives ignore the snow.

Sam lets the rumor fly. Within ten minutes, everyone has heard the rumor and hopes it's true. Five minutes after that, Sam tells the lower manager that the workers would be pleased with a three o'clock closing. The manager passes this information to the executives' administrative assistant.

Shortly thereafter, the chief executive announces the decision. Everybody is pleased. The top grape tactic works again.

To employ the Top Grape Tactic, identify the top grape in your organization as well as the middle grapes who feed them information. Note that this tactic's effectiveness can be magnified when combined with Walking Encyclopedia.

CHAPTER NINE

MMTs to Help You with Project Management

The best way to do work is to do it right the first time.

MANAGEMENT SAYS COMPLETE YOUR job on time, and within budget. Quality management says do the job right the first time. What is the difference? If you pressure people and reward them for getting the job done on time and within budget, they will meet budget and schedule goals, but at what cost?

As discussed in the previous chapter under "The PDCA Process," there is a concept called "cost of quality" which defines the cost of doing the job cheaply and quickly versus doing the job excellently. To review: there are three costs in the "cost of quality" formula: The cost of production; the cost of determining whether the job was done as specified; and the cost of failure, which is the cost of correcting problems uncovered after completion.

In the early days of computing, when programmers tested their own code, the cost of failure almost always exceeded the cost of writing the code. Even today, the cost of failure can be huge, as it was in the case of the faulty airplanes, which crashed because a new flight control system didn't receive adequate quality testing.

Quality management principles state that if you force people to complete their work on time and within budget, you are telling them to compromise quality if you must to meet the budget and deadline. They don't use the word *cheat*, but all incentives are based on deadlines and budgets rather than quality.

One of Dr. W. Edwards Deming's 14 Quality Principles can be paraphrased as *do not set goals*. Why this principle? If you pay your child to get an A grade, they will cheat to get that incentive, like using a generative text artificial intelligence to write papers for them.

As an auditor, I noticed that to meet a year-end sales goal, sales staff members would ask their best customers to buy something they did not need in December and then return it in January. This would help their sales reps meet or exceed goals and perhaps get a bonus.

When I was planning to build a home for my family, I met with a builder. My question to her was, "How much is it going to cost?" I wanted exact costs under a fixed-price contract.

The builder responded, "I can give you a fixed-price contract, and I will build it for that amount, but to do that I might have to cut some corners."

"What type of corners?"

"Well, if the price of wood goes up, I'll have to buy cheaper appliances, or only use one coat of paint instead of two, to meet my cost constraints."

"What other options do I have?"

"If you want a fixed-price contract? None. But if you'll let me have a cost plus 15 percent contract, I won't need to cut corners. I can control costs by purchasing supplies on sale and eliminate unnecessary parts of the plan if I find them. That way I can usually build a house below my estimate. Which sounds like a better deal? In one you control the cost. In the other you control quality."

I took the cost-plus contract, and never had a problem with the house.

Project management is a processes, not an art form. An artist may use different techniques and processes for each artwork they do. Project management requires an established process that is repeated every time. One good process has four parts, covered in Chapter Eight under "The PDCA Process." Good project management assumes first, that your workers are competent to do their jobs and second, the company culture encourages loyalty. Unhappy workers can lead to poor craftwork.

Completing your work with excellence is best done with flexible budgets and schedules. Targets, yes, a defined completion date if needed, but workers need the ability to make changes when it's advantageous to the customer. The MMTs in this chapter will help you produce high customer satisfaction.

MBWA: Management By Walking Around
Workers' gossip can often be more valuable
than executive reports.

There are two methods of communication in organizations: formal and informal. Formal methods are specified by the organization and include status reports, policy papers, and memos. Informal communications normally originate with lower-level employees and include scuttlebutt, complaints, and rumors. Neither method can be counted on to be reliable. A good manager will use both.

Fred Smith, CEO of Federal Express, would often eat lunch in the company cafeteria with employees of all levels. Smith had no agenda. Just by listening to the conversation going on around him he learned a lot from his employees' perspectives about how the company was doing.

Too many times, the information presented to one's boss is slanted in the direction of what the boss wants to hear, for example, a project status report might omit problems. *Slanted* often means that someone other than you is to blame for the delay, or that the project could stay on schedule by eliminating parts of the project such as quality testing. Note that this approach did not work well for the aircraft company.

Unofficial information is often less reliable than official information. What is important about reliable information, regardless of type, is the correct us of the information, which is the responsibility of the manager. If you are the manager, sending your boss incorrect information can cause your boss not only to distrust your reports; they will no longer trust you. Trust once lost is hard to recover.

My background in accounting has taught me to, as President Ronald Reagan said of negotiating with Russia, "trust but verify." That is, believe what someone tells you, but verify from other sources that what you were told is true.

As an examiner for the Malcolm Baldrige National Quality Award Program, I was taught to verify whether what management said about quality was actually put into practice. In quality terms, that meant "walking the talk." To verify management was walking the talk I would ask employees at all levels in the organization some questions:

- What is the company's quality policy?
- How important is quality in performing your job?
- What is the name of the company president?
- Is there anyone in the organization who will listen to your ideas and complaints?

It did not take me long to find out whether management's heart was truly in quality, or if it was in profits, goals, and schedules.

In today's business culture, if you want to talk to your boss you must go to your boss's office. Of course you know where that is. But as a consultant, I remember asking a manager where one of his employees' workstations was. He said, "I don't know." That's sad. Managers should know where their people are.

I suggested to the president of a hospital, who sat at her desk all day every day, to get up and walk around the hospital and talk to the medical administrative staff wherever they worked—just everyday chitchat.

After a week she said to me, "Thank you for forcing me to walk around the hospital. I learned a lot, and will be making some changes."

This is a tactic many consultants use—talk to low-level employees not only about what the problems are, but also how those problems can be solved. As noted in Chapter Six under "Identify Areas of Improvement," the people doing the work often are best positioned to provide this information. Managers would do well to collect it.

There are three secrets to effectively manage by walking around:

1. The manager of the project, department, or business area for which informal information is wanted must be the one walking around.
2. The manager walking around must interact with all levels of employees.
3. There cannot be any agenda or notes taken during the walk.

Why are these three secrets important? First, rarely does the senior manager walk around her area just to chat with subordinates. Workers might feel honored that a high-level manager would stop and talk to them, but only if they believe the manager is authentically trying to connect and learn. Second, by visiting workers in their own areas, managers can talk with them as colleagues, because the manager is not in the power position— that is, their office. Third, without an agenda, the conversation is considered just a random stop, thus a subordinate will feel free to talk.

What do you do with the information collected during your walk? When I walked around as a consultant, the people I talked to were usually eager to tell me what their departments needed. They did not want credit for their ideas—they just wanted their job to be easier and more meaningful. If the manager is relaxed and authentic, people will talk. If they think a manager is spying on them or has an ulterior motive, they will not talk. If they feel the manager genuinely wants to get to know the workers, they will talk. All the manager has to do is listen. Here are some sample questions you can ask your subordinates when you are walking around:

- What is your job?
- How do you like what you do?
- How do you like your employer?
- What is stopping you from doing a better job?
- What do you do when you're not working?

Rarely will they talk about their boss or colleagues. Most employees, when talking to a higher level boss, will discuss their job conditions, office culture, the future direction of the organization, and any impediments to doing their job. Discussions are usually positive, mixed with some personal information. Managers should not rely on the correctness of what they are being told, but rather looking for trends. For example, if most workers in a department say that what's holding them back is a lack of better tools, then an evaluation of replacement tools is warranted.

The key element of the Managing by Walking Around Tactic is not that the manager is seen—it's that the workers are heard.

Talk to People's Faces, Not Only to Their Computers
With computers you only get words;
face-to-face you get emotions.

A young man was talking with his aging father, who had just returned from the bank. "Dad, it's so much easier to do your banking on your phone. They have an app so you don't have to go to the branch to make your deposits."

Before his father could reply, the son rambled on. "And I've noticed you go to the grocery store three times a week. It must take a lot of time driving there and walking up and down the aisles. You could save time by ordering your groceries online and having them delivered. Same thing with dinner. Why do you go to the restaurant instead of having food delivered? I can help you download the app—"

"Son"—the father held up a hand—"I know you're trying to help, but I *like* going to the bank; they know me there, and it gets me out of the house. And I prefer to do my own shopping. Walking up and down the aisles is good safe exercise, and I like to choose my own produce and read labels before I buy. And I go to restaurants because I like being around people. Sometimes I meet my friends there, and sometimes other folks who are eating alone will ask to join me. It's not just about the food; dining out is an experience I enjoy."

"Oh, wow. I never saw it that way. I like to use my phone for everything."

"Well, there are times for that. Sometimes it is more efficient to order through an app or send an email. But as for me, I enjoy talking with people face-to-face."

We started our business in 1980 when I was fifty. We had a computer for accounting, and an electric typewriter for writing documents. People talked to each other by visiting each other's offices.

Then, in what seemed a short time, we reached a point where two people sitting in cubicles in the same office would text each other rather than walking over to the other person's cubicle.

At restaurants, we see every person at a table on their cell phones for most of their meal. We take courses online and buy products online. The word *talk* has been replaced by the word *text*. What happened?

The world has changed, starting with babies playing with electronic toys, to college graduates who have a difficult time giving oral presentations. The ability of students to read cursive has declined, so messages must be printed or typed. We had to change with the times, reminding ourselves "it is what it is."

There is a significant difference between texting and talking. An article in *USA Today* on August 23, 2023, "Relationships—Is texting a great way to have meaningful conversations?" stated that within relationships, texting leads to many misunderstandings because it can be hard when reading words to understand what the sender really meant. Facial expressions, body language, and tone of voice are all absent.

When supervisor and subordinates are communicating, the following topics are better addressed in face-to-face discussions:

- Performance or behavior issues, up to and including termination
- Explaining what you want done
- Correcting or mentoring a weakness
- Difficulties between coworkers
- Personal matters

In the case of instructions or disciplinary actions, a follow-up in writing may be advisable, but only after a face-to-face discussion has produced mutual understanding.

The difficulty with talking is that it is harder if you're an introvert or dislike confrontation. To improve your ability to have meaningful conversations, first improve your ability to listen to be sure what you hear is what the speaker means. Second, learn to be at ease while talking. To be more at ease, consider taking a public speaking class, or practice long conversations with friends. Also practice how to have difficult conversations when speaking one on one. The above-referenced *USA Today* article offered a five-step process to have an effective face-to-face conversation:

1. Prepare what you want to accomplish during your conversation.

2. Use "I feel" messaging to keep the focus on how you feel rather than on the other person's action or inaction.
3. Consider what is your most important message, and build your talk to illustrate that message.
4. Pause often to give your listener time to respond. If you feel tense, stop and take a breath or ask for a time out.
5. Specify boundaries by listing beforehand the topics you will not discuss.

Remember, talking is not stodgy and texting is not trendy. Talk when you should talk and text when you should text.

Turn the Herd
If your project is on the brink of disaster,
you can salvage a victory by turning the herd.

Of all the tactics for saving a project from disaster, the Turn the Herd Tactic is the most admired. It's a grandstand play and doesn't happen every day. In fact, you may only experience it a few times—maybe only once—in your career. If you can pull it off, it will bring a sense of satisfaction you'll never forget.

The Alabama football team was tied with rival Auburn on the 40-yard line with one second left. Alabama decided they had nothing to lose by kicking for a field goal in winning the game. If the kick missed, they would go into overtime.

The Auburn coach wanted to turn the herd for a win. He guessed that the Alabama coach would put his largest players on the line so the kick could not be blocked.

So he put his fastest player in the end zone, hoping the kick would fall short, and the Auburn player could run past Alabama's giant lineman.

The kick was short. The Auburn player ran for a touchdown. The Auburn coach and the runner were both carried off the field on other players' shoulders. The Auburn coach was a hero at Auburn then, and still is today, for turning that herd.

One key event can turn a situation around. Can this happen in business? Yes. Does it happen in business? Yes. But to turn the herd you must know the right time to turn the herd.

Katie Clever was a project manager on an important accounting project. The due date was rapidly approaching, but the project was stalled because those whose approval was needed for the next phase would not give it. They demanded Katie write what she thought was an unnecessary status update so another department would approve a substantial amount of overtime. Katie couldn't get the approvals in time to finish the project by the due date.

She needed to turn the herd. So, employing the "It Is Easier to Get Forgiveness Than Permission Tactic," she restarted the project without writing the update or getting the overtime approval.

Her team completed the project on time with minimal overtime.

In management's eyes, Katie was a hero, and all was forgiven about using overtime without prior approval.

Most people get their vision about turning the heard from watching western movies. In the movies, the cowboy wears a white hat and rides a white horse. He charges the heard from the opposite direction, firing both pistols wildly. The herd turns just before the cliff. In real life, the cowboy would be eating a hamburger from the dead cattle.

The way to turn the herd is to turn the leaders. If you can make them lead, the rest of the herd will follow. That's the way it is in business.

Let's observe Ken Census as he turns the herd on an assignment from his boss, Tim Tough. The assignment is to organize and run the office annual year-end party.

Tom doesn't want to run the party himself because it has always been a "must come, no fun" event. Those who ran it in the past had their careers ended.

Since Ken's situation is desperate, he knows he has to turn the herd to stay in the running for a promotion. Before making his move to turn the herd, he follows the three conditions vital to his success:

Become part of the herd. Ken sympathized with the rest of the cattle, joining them in uttering such expressions as "I hate these parties," and "why me?" or "why don't they just give us money instead?" Old Ken was trotting right alongside the rest of the beefers. Even though he was the planner of the event, he sounded like a victim.

Move to the head of the herd. Ken became the chief griper of the group. He told his boss he didn't have enough time, enough talent, or enough money to put on a successful party. Since Ken complained the most, his boss reminded him. "You're the boss of the party; do whatever you can within your budget."

Make the project unique. Ken thought long and hard about this. The annual office party had always been held at a restaurant, where there was no room to move around. This inhibited activity and conversation. He would instead hold a catered party at his home, with a tent in his big backyard. Nice move, Ken. Since this has never been tried before, it could not be compared to any other office party. It was unique. Ken was ready to turn the herd.

Ken started out slowly. He began to say, "You know, the party just might turn out to be tolerable this year."

Later he told his boss, "I think the troops will have fun." Since everyone really wanted to have a good time, Ken's mood was contagious. After all, he was the biggest griper. Ken thought it might work out . . . it just might.

The herd started to follow Ken and turn from despair to delight. Ken had the ball and was running for a touchdown.

If you stop to think about it, all kinds of situations that look bleak at first suddenly look better when seen from a different perspective.

Remember the dress you didn't care to buy until your husband said, "Honey, you look great in that dress." You bought it even though it cost $250.

How often has a child hated his toy until an older sibling said, "That's a great toy! I wish I had one."

These changes of perception happened because someone turned the herd.

Focus On The Process, Not The Outcome
You cannot control the result,
but you can control the method.

Many bosses give you an assignment that includes a schedule and budget, emphasizing the importance of meeting the schedule and budget and not on the work required to achieve the desired outcome. Employees believe they will be evaluated by meeting deadlines and budgets, so they focus on cutting costs and working quickly.

Dr. W. Edward Deming believed that when employees are judged by budgets and schedules, they will cheat to achieve those objectives. How do they cheat? They look for ways to eliminate components of their work requirements, and they skimp on checking the accuracy of their work to meet the deadlines.

Workers who emphasize quality rather than budgets and timelines do it by using proven processes. In most cases, by emphasizing quality, the workers will still meet the budget and schedule objectives.

My wife and I wanted to raise a large amount of money to build an athletic complex for a new church school. It took several years to get approval, because the church's experience in using golf events to raise money was that they could charge up to $100 per person. That wouldn't be enough to build an athletic complex.

With severe reservations, they gave us permission to have a fundraising golf event. We put together a group of school parents who knew how to run fundraising events. At the first meeting of that committee, they asked two questions: first, what is the budget?, and second, how much money are we expected to raise?

Our answers surprised them. We said there will be no budget: your mission is to put together a world-class golf event, and you are not responsible for how much money can be raised.

Anyone hearing us in a business school would be shocked. But our reasoning was that budgets constrain workers from doing the right thing. And organizers cannot control how much money a fundraising event will bring in. We wanted our committee to follow the processes they knew would work for putting on a fundraising event, without budgetary or scheduling constraints.

As chairs of the event, we were responsible for how much money would be raised. Did this quality-focused approach work? YES. We raised over $100,000 the first year and much more in the following years.

Who else follows the quality approach? Tom Landry, ex-coach of the Dallas Cowboys. Landry told me that for the Cowboys, he had eleven processes for offense, and eleven approaches for defense. One process for each player. Landry accepted responsibility for winning, and he gave the players a game plan for winning. All Landry asked of his players was to follow his plan and play their position. Landry's approach enabled them to win more games than any other NFL team for years.

Nick Saban, coach of the University of Alabama football team, once said that for his first twenty years as a football coach he focused on the outcome, that is, winning. To win, he developed a coaching style that was all about winning. After losing many games that he thought he should have won, he, like Tom Landry changed his focus. He said, "The process is really what you have to do day in and day out to be successful."

Saban said he tried to "define the standard that we want everybody to sort of work toward," with elements such as "being responsible for your own self-determination, having a positive attitude, having great work ethic, having discipline to be able to execute on a consistent basis, whatever it is you're trying to do, those are the things that we try to focus on, and we don't try to focus as much on the outcomes as we do on being all that you can be."

This required a new coaching approach, but with that he became one of the coaches with the most wins in college football.

How can a manager focus on the process and not the outcome? This can only happen if his organization has a process that works, so he can rely on it to get his job done. The key point is that it *works*: if it does not work it can hinder getting the job done.

For example, if you buy a bicycle, it comes with a process for assembly. Some people don't believe a process is necessary, and only care about getting a bike assembled. They dump all the pieces on the floor and start sticking parts together. If they fail to complete the assembly, they have to start over again—maybe this time they'll even read the instructions.

Those who believe in processes read the process and follow it. They trust the assembly process developed by the maker of the bike will work.

Effective processes start with a **Plan** for assembling the bike. The instructions tell you to count all the parts to assure they are all in fact there and to gather the tools you will need. Then you are ready to **Do** what the instructions tell you to. After assembling the bike, you will **Check** that the bike works, and that all the parts are now incorporated into it. If something is wrong, you will **Act** to fix the problem.

Sound familiar? Yep, that's the previously mentioned PDCA Process, the components of which form a process that works.

How does Tom Landry coach the Dallas Cowboys using a PDCA Process?

Planning is a very time-consuming part of winning a game. He must have a schedule of who and where he plays, he must have the tools to play the game and a field to practice on, he must have techniques like training regimens and briefings to prepare his players, he has personnel like specialized coaches, and a playbook from which he will develop a literal game plan for each game.

Next, he will execute the **Do** component by using his tools, his players, and his game plan as they take the field.

He'll place a quality coach in the upper stands to **Check** and report how the plays worked or failed (a new concept in football). For example, if they had a play to run through a specific tackle on the other team, but the opposition put a 350-pound guard in that position, Landry's planned play could not work.

At half time, Landry and his coaches will **Act** by substituting another play.

Why did Tom Landry tell his players they were not responsible for winning a game, just for playing their positions and following the game plan? Because before coaching football, Landry was an industrial engineer and was used to the PDCA Process.

Don't get so involved with the outcome that you neglect to use your processes to achieve that outcome.

Put the *I* back in Team

It Is Important to Identify the Imperative of each Individual.

The traditional team management strategy is stated on signs posted in many businesses: "There is no *I* in team." This message confuses anyone appointed to join a team.

This is how many team members feel when they are assigned: If there is no *I* in team, what am I supposed to do during team meetings? Do I have a role? Why was I appointed? If I work hard and make positive contributions to the team, will I receive recognition for my work? What type of training will I receive? And if my committee assignment infringes on my ability to complete the job I am being paid to do, will my supervisor give me more time to do my regular job? Am I here to contribute as an individual, or is this just a groupthink, mob-mentality exercise?

Most of us have a love-hate relationship with teams. We love our sports teams, especially from our alma maters, but few of us genuinely enjoy having to participate in team activities in school or at work. I have had the best of times as a member of a team that accomplished much more than the sum of each person's input; however, I have also had the worst of times when poor group dynamics actually diminished each team member's contribution.

I have concluded, after thousands of hours sitting through team meetings, that there are very, very few great teams. I am convinced, however, that great teams can and do exist, and that it is possible to transform a good team into a great team. We need to make an effort to create great teams, because teams are becoming increasingly important in today's business culture.

The mentor who taught me great team dynamics was Tom Landry, who was coach of the Dallas Cowboys from 1960 to 1988 and led the Cowboys to many championships. Tom explain to me how he built a world-class football team.

He said a team is not a democracy but rather a dictatorship. He was the dictator; he would listen to everybody, but at decision time he made the decisions.

Everybody on his team had a responsibility to fulfill the role they were given and practice until he was proficient at performing that role. He said it was not the responsibility of each team member to win the game, but to fulfill their role. As coach, Tom was responsible for the game plan and bore full responsibility for winning or losing a game.

If a player fulfilled his role, he was rewarded, regardless of the game's outcome. If a player was having an off day, he was replaced.

Tom created what he called a quality control coach. That coach was located at the top of the grandstands and looked for ways to improve the team's performance in the second half of the game.

Granted, a business team is not a football team, but Tom and I discussed how his approach to team building could be applied to a business committee. This section will explain how.

Let's look at another example of a sports team that's more similar to a business committee. A Little League baseball team is starting, and each team in the league must have a coach. A friend volunteers you to be the coach of the Cellar Dwellers. You have never coached, but you have played baseball so you accept the position.

Without conducting tryouts, you select your son and his friends to join the team, along with some boys whose parents want their kids to grow up and be professional ball players. Those other parents will regularly tell you when and how to use their kids throughout the season.

Your only strategic planning is determining when the team will practice and for how long. With no structured practices and little direction, the team loses their first game, and every game thereafter.

Now imagine how the league-leading Yankees approach team activities. At the start of each season, they recruit a coach with baseball coaching experience who has proven he can win. The coach organizes a camp to test players for each position. He recruits the best players to join his team and puts each player in a position they are well-suited for. Players practice their positions and improve their skills.

The coach develops a game plan and motivates the individuals to play their positions to the best of their ability. The coach states he is responsible for winning, and if each player plays hard and follows his game plan, the team should win.

No surprise, the Yankees win the league championship.

What lessons can you learn about business committees from the Little League Yankees? The committee chairperson must be skilled at running a committee and want to fill the position so the committee's goal can be accomplished.

Each committee member should be selected for a specific purpose. Everyone on the committee should know its mission of the committee and what metrics will be used to determine when or whether the goal is met.

The chairperson needs to prepare a plan detailing what processes will be used to achieve the committee's goals. Once the goals are reached, each committee member that contributed should be rewarded.

With Tom Landry's help, I developed a seven-step process for organizing and running committees:

Step One: Identify the task that management wants the committee to perform, and determine by what metrics the committee will will use to show they have completed the task successfully.

Step Two: Appoint a chairperson who has the motivational skills to guide the committee to a successful conclusion.

Step Three: Define the skills committee members will need, and then find and appoint individuals with those skills to the committee. The members must want to serve and have the support of their supervisors to allow them to time to serve.

Step Four: Prepare the team members to fulfill their rules by providing all the background information needed to do the task—including what challenges they must overcome to succeed—and give them a plan to follow to achieve success.

Step Five: Ensure each team member fulfills their role and works with other team members until the committee has reached a consensus for making a recommendation to management.

Step Six: Present the recommendation to management with a high-level plan for successful implementation.

Step Seven: Appoint one or more committee members to oversee the implementation of the committee's recommendation.

It is important to note that, at all costs, you must avoid putting these people on your committee:

Dominator—never stops talking, uses filibustering, interrupting, and asking to speak

Bystander—does not want to attend and mentally checks out of meetings

My-Way Commander—believes there is only one way to meet the committee's objectives and will not consider any alternative

Escalator—makes a simple objective complex

Detailer—wants every discussion to address minor issues first

Destroyer—has a hidden agenda that has nothing to do with the committee's objective

Will management be excited to implement the seven-step process for committees? Probably not. It's much easier to just appoint a committee chairperson, tell that person what is wanted, and leave everything that follows to chance.

So how can Putting The I Back In Team Tactic help you manage your managers to obtain great teams? If you are assigned to be a team chairperson, use this seven-step process. If it is successful, share the seven-step committee process and promote its future use. Or, if you are assigned to a team, ask your team chairperson to use this process.

The Trial Balloon Tactic
A weak swimmer who swims with the tide will beat a strong swimmer who swims against the tide.

To spot rip currents at the beach, a lifeguard watches for seaweed and sea foam being swept away from the shore.

To determine wind speed and direction, a golfer picks a few pieces of grass and throws some up into the wind.

To determine what color to paint a room, a decorator puts a small patch of each color they're considering on the wall to try them out.

Such tests cost very little, while their value can be very high. For example, if the decorator paints an entire room to determine whether the client will like the color, and the client doesn't like it, they will have to repaint the entire room.

Samples are the simplest form of trial balloon. Other methods are more complex.

Let's follow the path of George Goodman as he leads a committee to select a new location for his company's corporate headquarters. George knows if he finds the right location, he'll be rewarded with a new corporate suite.

George assumes he will need a lot of facts to support his decision. Therefore he studies the cost of real estate, the tax structure of various communities, the employment picture, prevailing wage scales in each area, comparative studies of projected wages and tax structures over the next ten years, and thirteen other factors that lesser folk would not even have considered, and much more.

Based on his own proprietary, scientifically developed algorithm, George runs all these facts run through his computer. The indisputable results show the corporate headquarters should be moved from downtown New York City to Bergen County, New Jersey. With confidence, George presents his facts—displayed on colorful charts produced during weeks and weekends of work— to corporate management. The benefits of moving to Bergen County, New Jersey, are indisputable.

How does management react? They shoot holes in his report. They wonder out loud how George could've come up with such a ridiculous choice as Bergen County, New Jersey.

Where did George go wrong? Did he failed to consider all the factors?

Yes. George neglected to find out which way the tide was running. Our hard-working committee chairman made a fatal mistake—he went against the tide. He took management at its word, thinking that what they wanted was a thorough analysis of the facts to logically decide on the best location. What they really wanted were facts to support an illogical decision.

How could George have found out what management wanted? He could have sent up a trial balloon, the same way a meteorologist releases a weather balloon to see what way the wind is blowing. If before George released his report he had released a trial balloon for Bergen and it was shot down, he would've known he was running against the tide.

What should George have done? If he released his trial balloon and it was shot down, he would realize that only a damn fool would make a recommendation that had already been rejected. He could use the feedback from the trial balloon's failure to determine a better course of action.

He might have learned that most of the homes of his corporation's executives were in Stamford, Connecticut, and that those managers were already complaining about the long commute to New York City. That would show him which way the tide was running, and he could have used his facts to prove that the best location for the new corporate headquarters would be in Stamford. Or, if George had wanted to fight the tide, he could have tried to do so by using the Turn the Herd tactic.

What lessons does the trial balloon teach? First, if you want to be successful with your proposal or assignment, find out which way the tide is going and swim with it. Second, while swimming against the tide is not always fatal, it always creates hardship and makes success more difficult.

If the direction of your current project has you in confusion, send up some trial balloons to see which way the wind is blowing in your organization.

Finish What You Start
The readiness and excitement of starting a project must be matched by energy expended on finishing the project.

Ideas inspire action. But what counts is not the idea, but getting the thing done. The world is full of starters, but there are few finishers. All worthwhile achievements are the result of an idea, a start, and a strong finish—particularly the finish. There is no greater finale to a person's effort than the simple words, "It is finished."

Many think all that is needed to complete a project is initiative. But that is only one factor. Action must be sustained from beginning to end to be effective. The direct cause of most failures is lack of definite action. It is the predominating error in every walk of life.

Ask yourself, in your lifetime how many projects have you started but never completed? Failure to finish a project is not new, it is an age-old reality. Most miners looking for gold in California and Alaska stopped at digging or panning for gold because they hadn't found any. But the gold was there, to be found by those who persisted with continual action.

Many unfinished projects are dropped at a point where the project is close to 90 percent complete. Why? Those working on it lose interest, and want to move on. Why do they lose interest? Because the last few steps are often the hardest to complete.

When a sales representative pursues a sale, they start by opening a dialogue with the prospective clients. They take action by delivering samples or writing proposals. Then, as they draw close to the point of signing an order, they stop taking action and fail to close the deal. What happened? Perhaps the customer wanted another concession and the sales rep didn't have the stamina for negotiating. Or maybe a seemingly bigger prospect came along, and the sales rep redirected their attention.

In other cases, projects fail due to a lack of resources or planning, if not both.

Starting in 1816, the National Monument Committee in Scotland began planning a monument to commemorate those who died in the Napoleonic Wars. The government refused to fund the project, and the committee's attempt to get a grant from the church also failed. The committee nevertheless began construction of a Greek Parthenon-style structure in 1822, with a plan to collect private donations. But the money did not come in, and the project was abandoned in 1829 with only three of four sides completed.

Similarly, in Central Florida a Christian broadcaster began con-struction of a huge office and studio building in 2001. The devel-oper proudly stated that the project would *not* use any debt to finance the construction, but would be built out using only funds that were donated by the broadcaster's viewers. As of this writing, more than two decades later, the building is still not completed. It's known locally as the Eyesore on I4.

The course of least resistance is the road to the scrap heap. If you develop an idea and propose it to your managers, and they give you approval to begin, you must first know in your heart you are willing to do whatever is necessary to complete the project. You must believe in yourself and commit to completing the project. To succeed you must have determination and stamina to maintain a course of action.

CHAPTER TEN

Improve Your Competencies

These competencies include not only skills, but courage, confidence, and love of people.

IT IS IMPERATIVE TO grow in life. A wise old woman told me early in my marriage that if we didn't grow together, we would grow apart and end up divorced. Too many people feel that once they are out of school they can stop learning, and if more skills are needed their employer should not only pay for it, but give them time off to go to class. But each of us must take control of our own growth, whether in our personal lives or our professional lives.

When I was a teenager and picked up our landline telephone, the operator said, "Number please." Now on my cell phone I can call anywhere in the world and access approximately 90 percent of all the information in the world. How are you to keep up with the rapid growth of technology? Just say, "If it is going to be, it's up to me." Find out what you need and go get it, whether it's developing interpersonal skills, learning to write code, or finding out how artificial intelligence will affect your business.

The daughter of a close friend recently graduated from college. Listed on her resume were all her work skills, yet like many of her friends, she still cannot get a job. Many people do not realize the foundation on which you should build your skill set consists of Behavior, Confidence, Motivation, and Beliefs.

A past CEO of IBM said that when she hires a person, she doesn't care what school they graduated from or what skills they have, she wants someone who wants to learn, knows how to learn, and can put what they learned into practice.

When I am asked to help someone get a job, I tell them to downplay work skills, and present their strengths. The motto of my college was, "A workman who needs not to be ashamed," which is taken from the apostle Paul, who wrote, "Study to shew thyself approved unto God, a workman that needeth not to be ashamed, rightly dividing the word of truth" (2 Timothy 2:15, KJV). Not only should workers be unashamed, they should like their jobs and take pride in the products of their efforts. Expand that concept to talk about building relationships with coworkers and customers, how satisfying customers is very important to you, and your willingness to learn and apply what you learned on the job.

Learning should be a lifetime skill. Never stop learning, or you may find yourself looking for a job. The MMTs in this chapter represent a small sample of the skills you will need in the future.

No Pain, No Gain
Perfection comes at a price.

To do something because you are paid to do it entails little pain and little gain.

To put some extra effort into doing your job entails some pain and some gain.

To excel at your job entails much pain and much gain.

There are many reasons why someone undertakes a job, ranging from the basic need to support oneself and one's family to wanting to use all of one's abilities to be successful. Abilities include one's skill set and proficiency in applying them, knowing how work will be evaluated and achieving those objectives, and sustaining motivation.

In football, when a player puts all his effort into playing at full speed for sixty minutes, they say, "I left it all on the field." Jesus literally instructed us to go the extra mile when he said, "Whoever compels you to go one mile, go with him two" (Matthew 5:41, NKJV).

This tactic will be successful when at the end of a job you can say, "I've done my best." By doing your best you will achieve a level of performance far beyond what an average worker will achieve.

When a football player reports to training camp, they undergo the extensive physical training they will need to prepare them for competition. Their training prepares them to play the position they have been assigned. They practice for weeks before competing, and continually between games. They must also learn discipline, study the playbook, and watch their opponents in films so they will know how their opponents play the game. All this for a sixty-minute game. Now ask yourself, compared to a football player, how prepared am I to do the job I have been assigned?

What does being prepared to do your job mean? If you are expected to work an eight-hour day, how many of those eight hours will be spent gossiping, taking coffee breaks, and planning your life after work? Before you start work, do you know exactly what you are being asked to do?

Do you know what skills you need? If you do not have those skills, or are not proficient using those skills, how do you plan to compensate for your lack of skills? Are you sure the people who will help you are competent to do what is needed?

Do you have a quality control plan for evaluating your completed work to assure you have done all that is needed?

Are you prepared to tell your boss if you are in trouble meeting your objectives, and to ask for more help rather than letting poor work go into distribution?

In any job there are things you can control, and things you cannot control. If you are required to prepare a weekly report, you can control when you file that report and what information it contains.

If you need to do more work than you will be paid for, you can choose whether to work extra hours on your own, or not put in extra unpaid time. But if your staff is paid hourly, they need to be paid time and one-half for extra hours worked over their eight-hour day: that is required and you cannot choose otherwise.

If you need more training, and your employer will not pay for it, you can choose to pay from your own funds for the course you need. I am always surprised at how many employees expect their employer to pay for all continuing education, and are not willing to pay for their own professional development. If you lack a skill, for example, using pivot tables in spreadsheets, are you willing to pay with your own money for a course to learn that skill? That might be painful, but the results can improve your job performance and prospects.

If during the execution of a task there is something you think you should do that is not part of what you are paid to do, there is pain involved in doing it, but there is also something to be gained. If there is someone you do not like on your project, but you feel that making an effort to improve the relationship is worthwhile, it can be painful to smile at that person and thank them for what they have done, but by doing so you may turn someone who does not want you succeed into someone who will help you succeed.

When you are faced with doing something you are not required to do, but you think you should do, how do you decide whether or not to undergo the pain to get future gain? Visualize doing your assignment as sending products down a series of conveyor belts. If at some point in the assembly line one of the conveyor belts breaks down, the products stop moving.

The same analogy holds for any work assignment. If someone, or some process, inserts an impediment that interrupts the workflow, the time to complete the job will be increased. For example, if you need a supervisor's approval to move to the next step in a process, but that supervisor is on vacation, you would have to stop working and wait for the supervisor to return to restart the process.

Our answer to this quandary is this: Do whatever is the right thing to do, for your organization and the people involved. Whether to do it or not is your decision. Consider whether you are willing to accept the pain (which might include punishment) to achieve the gains for yourself, your organization, and your colleagues and clients.

Appraise Yourself Before Being Appraised
Your performance review is too important to let your boss control it.

I have done hundreds of performance reviews, and I agree with Dr. W Edwards Deming when he said that performance reviews are the most destructive activity any employee is subjected to.

To my knowledge, very few bosses like to give performance reviews, and almost every employee hates them. Employees rightfully hate these reviews for two reasons. First, you have to wait fifty-two weeks to find out how you're doing. Second, reviews tend to focus on shortcomings, spending most of the time talking about what you did wrong instead of on your strengths and how to get even better at what you do well. Most employees spend what little time they have during a performance defending them-selves, with no time or interest in the staff member telling their boss what they are good at. After being beat up by their boss, some feel there is no hope. They thank the boss for their sugges-tions and get out of there.

I was never trained in how to conduct a performance review. The method I followed was to repeat how I how been reviewed by my boss, and I remember how painful it was. This is a very poor way to learn how to do a performance review, especially if you're modeling someone who doesn't know how to do one properly. It is like asking an alcoholic who's not yet in recovery how to stop drinking.

When I first became a supervisor, I did not look forward to conducting performance reviews, but I tried to make it a positive experience for my staff. I failed. My staff did not like my reviews any better than I did. The subjects I had to discuss with them were: Did they get along well with their coworkers and custom-ers? Did they follow the work rules? Did they complete their work on time and within budget? What were their weaknesses and how can they improve them? What they wanted to know was how did I rate them and why? How much of a raise were they going to get? And what do they need to do to get promoted?

One of my better staff members, John, came to my office for his annual performance review. I shut the door, but before I could start my appraisal, John asked me if he could give me some helpful information for the review. I was not prepared for his comments. John outlined what he had done the past year, with chart and graphs, documenting how he had helped me and the company. His statistics were difficult to refute.

When I had my chance, I went through my performance appraisal checklist, and was embarrassed by some of the negative comments on it. For example, some coworkers though he was too aggressive in using new approaches.

When we both finished, I did not know what to say. All I said was thank you, give me time to assess what you gave me. I didn't know what he had been doing for a year.

I concluded the following:

1. I needed to know more about what my staff was doing for me and our company. In John's case, I was only was prepared to rate him on things not related to the performance of his day-to-day job.

2. Performance appraisals need to be done much more than once per year. Dr. Deming says you should evaluate your staff daily: tell them what they doing well and where they need to improve.

3. Good business practices state that we should find out what people are doing right, and help them do more of that, instead of dwelling on what they did wrong.

4. Encourage staff members to do a performance appraisal on themselves before the formal review, then get their review before the formal meeting, and incorporate that into their assessment. A small number of organizations ask coworkers to evaluate each other.

The following four practices will make your performance review positive and fair:

1. Spend a lot of time preparing for the review, because your future may depend of how well prepared and assertive you are.

2. Develop a list of things your boss might say about you that you will not agree with. This concept is a classic sales technique. For example, when you want to buy a car, the salesperson knows how much they will sell the car for, and if you say that price is too much, the salesperson will offer a better deal on financing, or offer to add accessories at no extra cost. They can do this because they have anticipated potential objection and developed solutions in advance. You can do that with your boss.

3. Prepare as many statistics as possible about your work, for example, how many nights and Saturdays you put in to get your job done, innovations you proposed that were successful, or projects you took on outside the scope of your job description. Keep a journal or create a document listing your successes and update it throughout the year to help with this step.

4. Thank your boss for their recommendations and concerns, then ask for a time when you can tell your boss what you will do, or why you disagree with some of their comments.

By taking control of your own performance review, you can take one of the most harmful business practices and turn it to your advantage.

The Golden Rule
Treating others as you wish to be treated is good business.

Many years ago, I wrote a book for Christian students titled *Growing Up with No Rules*. Teachers and students both loved the book: the students didn't like following rules, and the teachers had a difficult challenge to get their students to follow rules. The book didn't say, "All rules are good," but many are for safety, such as a rule not to touch a hot stove. Other rules make your life better, like obeying traffic signals. The book concluded by asking the reader, "If you only had to follow one rule, what would that rule be?"

The book's answer is a teaching commonly known as The Golden Rule: "So in everything, do to others what you would have them do to you . . . " (Matthew 7:12, NIV). Teachers wanted to use the book to explain why there are rules, but couldn't use a Christian book in public schools.

The Golden Rule Society, which has been in existence for more than fifty years, rephrases the Golden Rule this way: "Treat others the way you want to be treated—truthfully, with dignity and respect." If you're a manager (or spouse or parent), do you want to be treated as someone who will be truthful to others? Do you want to be treated with dignity and respect? If you want others to do that for you, you must also do that for them. A leader does not have to be liked, but must be respected. Practicing the Golden Rule is the key to getting respect.

I used to visit Paris Island, the marine training base in Beaufort County, South Carolina, to watch the recruits graduate after weeks of intensive training. At the end of the graduation ceremony, the recruits are told, "You are now a marine," and the cheering is always very loud. Why? After weeks of brutal training, they earned the right to be respected Marines. It is a life-changing experience for each graduate.

Do you feel trust, dignity, and respect from your coworkers and family?

There are many ways a manager can lead subordinates. If you place the types of leader ship on a spectrum, at one end would be managing by the Golden Rule and at the other end would be managing by fear. Fear may work to make people do what the boss wants, but it will never create loyalty.

Bobby Bowden, the former football coach of Florida State University, had the best record of any Florida State coach. He stated that his first job was to help his players become great men, and second was to be their coach.

The Golden Rule can help your career in three ways:

- You avoid becoming a manager who manages by fear and instead become the type of person people want to associate with.
- You avoid getting a bad reputation, for example, as one who plays favorites, or who punishes subordinates who challenge you about what you want them to do or for having opinions different from yours.
- You build a good relationship with your coworkers by being kind honest and respecting people, which helps both you and themselves be successful.

The best way to convert an enemy or someone who holds a grudge against you is to follow the Golden Rule—it's hard for someone to dislike you if you're happy and kind and look after the best interest of others.

In Victor Hugo's novel *Les Miserables*—and the Broadway musical of the same name—the lead character, Jean Valjean, after escaping from jail, is hunted down by Javert, a police officer with a grudge against Valjean, who has gotten away from him in the past. When Valjean joins the rebels of the Paris Uprising, they have captured Javert, whom they plan to execute as a spy. Valjean offers to do this, but after taking Javert to a secluded place, lets him go. When they meet again, Javert vows to arrest Valjean, but later relents, because of the mercy Valjean showed him.

How do you find people who follow the Golden Rule?

One major entertainment corporation has perspective job applicants walk through a long path covered with many signs stating what the company expects from anyone they hire. At the end, they can take an interview. About 50 percent of those perspective applicants do not sit for an interview.

My wife and I went to a restaurant during its opening week. Halfway through dinner, we asked our server where he had worked before.

He answered, "I have never been a server before."

Surprised, I asked to see the manager. When he came to our table, I said, "You sent us a rookie server. Isn't that a risk?"

"I can teach anybody to serve in two days," he said. "I cannot teach anyone to be nice; therefore I hire people who like people." He looks for people who like people, who care about those they serve, and who want to satisfy customers. Those qualities are hard to find.

In my business, I hired a woman as a receptionist because she was kind, polite, and caring. She was great on the phone—one of the best I have ever heard. As a single mother, she occasionally had to take time off to be there for her children when they needed her. This did not happen very often, but it was too often for our office manager, so he fired her.

"Why?" I asked.

His response was, "In my opinion it is more important to be at work than to be a great receptionist."

Shortly after, I fired that manager. He did not care about his workers or our clientele. He never learned the Golden Rule.

The Baldrige National Quality Award Program was established by the US Department of Commerce in 1987 to identify corporations that excel in quality. The criteria for identifying world-class quality management systems was developed by the department and are used by examiners who measure how many of the criteria a candidate corporation meets. Examiners score each candidate on a scale of 0 to 1,000, and corporations that exceed 850 points are eligible to receive an award from the US president, on the condition that they share their quality management expertise with others.

The Golden Rule is not part of the Baldrige criteria, but as an examiner I felt many of the criteria support Golden Rule principles:
- What is the candidate's corporate vision and values?
- Do they have visionary leadership?
- Do they survey customers to help them drive excellence in all they do?
- Are employees valued?
- Do they manage by facts, not feelings?
- Are they socially responsible?
- How do senior leaders, including the CEO, guide and sustain the corporation and communicate with employees to encourage high performance?

Managers who apply the Golden Rule to their everyday work accept their coworkers for who they are and not who the manager wants them to be. Like Bobby Bowden, their first job is to make their coworkers better people and second to help them be better employees.

The Missing Tile
Insert deliberate flaws in your documents
to highlight quality control.

If you see a mosaic with one tile missing, your eye goes directly to the empty space where the missing tile should be. You cannot help it.

Conversely, sometimes errors can only be found when you know what to look for—the tile might not be missing, but wrong. Still, if you know to look for it, you can ensure the quality of your work.

Rock bands and other performers are notorious for placing outrageous demands in their contracts with venues, such as requiring a specific number of cans or bottles of a particular beverage to be placed in the dressing room. Although these contract riders seem frivolous, they play an important quality control function.

Van Halen, for example, famously requested that they be provided with a container of cholocate pieces with candy shells—but with no brown ones. As outlined in "No Brown M&Ms: What Van Halen's Insane Contract Clause Teaches Entrepreneurs," published by *Entrepreneur* on March 24, 2014, this seemingly fatuous request served an important function: ensuring that the venue's management had read and adhered to the entire contract.

Contracts for such performances often include specifications about the amount of weight that can be borne by the stage or the capacity of the electrical system: These are safety issues for the performers. So if the band members came into the venue and found brown-shelled chocolates—or none of the candy at all—they could tell the venue manager had not ensured that all of the contract's provisions had been met, and they could call for a complete check of all the other conditions to ensure the safety of their team. The candy pieces were their missing tile.

Using this tactic to improve your quality control competency is a two-step process: First, examine your work thoroughly to ensure there are no flaws. Second, intentionally remove something or insert a flaw. When the work is submitted to your managers, you can determine whether they are paying attention by whether they identify the missing tile.

Also keep in mind that many managers, if they can find one defect in your work, will stop looking for more, feeling they have done their job.

A lot of what I write is professionally edited. A fellow author asked, "How do you know the editor is doing a good job?"

My answer was, "I really don't know." So I asked him, "How could I know?"

He answered, "Put in some misspellings and other minor errors. If your editor finds and corrects them, you'll know they're doing a thorough job. If not, your editor edited too fast."

Although you would not want to insert a deliberate flaw into a work product that is about to go to your end user, you can use this technique earlier in the process when the product will come back to you, and you can use it on internal documents like memos and reports.

For example, rather than asking permission to take an action, you can send your manager an email saying you will take action unless they tell you not to. If they fail to respond, you will know they weren't paying attention, yet you will have cover for taking the action.

Here are some suggestions for tiles you can use for this purpose:
- Use incorrect terminology.
- Make errors in math calculations.
- Reference the wrong source.
- Misspell the names of individuals receiving your documents.
- Omit the names of individuals who contributed to the project.
- Omit an important piece of information, such as cost.

The process of identifying these flaws prior to the release of a document is called quality control, which probably uses a checklist. This checklist may be written down or not.

Early in my business, I was running seminars in cities throughout the USA. Our plan for our San Francisco seminar was to mail the brochures five weeks before the seminar. When the printed brochures arrived a few days late, we had a team ready to stuff, address, stamp, and mail them.

My wife noticed that *San Francisco* was misspelled on the brochure. Proofreading was part of her mental checklist for quality control.

"Mail them anyway," I said. "Time is short."

"No," she said, "the Quality Assurance Institute cannot do that!"

She was right—there was a tile missing. We reprinted the brochure, and even though they went out behind schedule, the seminar was still successful.

You do not need permission to use this tactic, and it can be an important one to employ if you are uncertain about whether your manager is paying full attention to your work. However, be forewarned that intentionally inserting flaws into your documents carries a risk of upsetting your recipient, in which case do a risk analysis based on what you know about your manager before using this tactic.

Circumventing Silos
Avoid having other departments delay your project.

When businesses are small, the few people that work there each wear many hats. At a small company, a treasurer might be responsible for income projections, paying invoices, and managing payroll. As organizations get bigger, those functions are separated for control purposes. These new self-contained functions are called silos—not the ones for storing grain, but standalone organizational departments like finance, accounts payable, and human resources. Each department or silo is given authority over its functions and is responsible for enforcing procedures related to those functions.

A project may be unable to move forward until it receives clearance from a relevant silo. For example, I once experienced a long delay in getting a payment; the silo rejected our payment request because we did not complete the necessary paperwork in full. Specifically, we left blank a field on the payment request form that did not apply to our request. Because we left the field empty instead of putting *N/A* in that slot, the payment request was rejected.

The problem with silos is that they are not concerned about the overall success of any project; they are focused on their department's success at enforcing the procedures they oversee. Most silos care more about doing what they are charged to do that about helping projects meet scheduled completion dates. This tactic is designed to minimize the impact a silo might have on your project.

Remember that each silo will take time to do what they are charged to do. The sooner you can deliver the information the silo requires, the greater the chance the silo will not delay your project. It can also be helpful to include in your work schedule the time the silo will need to approve you to continue working on your project.

It is important to understand the culture not only of your organization but also of each silo. In some cultures, silo managers will be flexible about getting you through the checkpoint, while others will not. If a silo has an inflexible manager, ask a staff member to help you complete that department's paperwork to the manager's requirements; most will offer some help.

Three tactics can help you circumvent silos or minimize the impact of getting approval to move forward:

1. Prior to the deadline to get approval from a silo, ask for permission to continue working until your request is approved.
2. Forget you need approval from the silo, and just keep working. If the silo says you're late getting your approval, tell them you forgot and are sorry and will get in your request ASAP— this works best if the silo is very busy.

3. Submit incomplete paperwork prior to the needed date; this will be returned to you. Keep working until you get the approval. Normally the silo will not know what you were doing.

Listen Actively
Be sure that what you heard is what the speaker meant.

Most people are involved in two types of conversation. One is social conversation about activities with family and friends. If something is required from you it normally is easy to accept or reject or modify. Social discussions do not require you to use formal listening practices.

The other is business or formal conversation in which the speaker will require you to do something for them. In both cases, most people do not listen actively. Therefore, they do not understand the meaning of what they heard or do what they are asked to do. Most people are never taught active listening, so their not knowing how to listen is unsurprising.

My six-year old son Scott rarely picked up his clothes and toys from the floor to put them where they belonged. One day after school, as he was going out to play, I said, "Scott, go to your room and clean up your mess, and do not leave your room until it's clean."

"Okay, Dad." He went off to clean up his room. Fifteen minutes later he returned. "It's all clean, Dad, can I go out to play now?"

I went to his room, and it looked clean—until I looked under the bed. All his junk was there. To me, the room wasn't clean, he had just moved his mess. But to Scott, it was clean.

What happened? Scott listened, but I did not communicate what I wanted in enough detail that Scott would know what I meant, not just what I said.

There are only a few listening practices one needs to master. Of these practices, the one that causes the most difficulty is giving your full attention to the person talking to you.

At another time, I told my daughter Debra, "You have been invited to Karen's birthday party today; be ready to go by three o'clock."

At three o'clock she wasn't even dressed.

What happened? All she heard was that she was invited to Karen's birthday party; after that, she stopped listening to tell me how happy she was to be going.

This is a common listening error: while you are talking, the other person stops listening and begins thinking about how to respond; therefore, they miss part of what you are saying.

Active listening is rarely taught. People believe it's an instinct, but it is actually a skill to be learned.

Active listeners follow these guidelines:

1. When someone is talking to you, prepare yourself to listen; free your mind of other thoughts.
2. Look the speaker in the eye, and watch their nonverbal communications, which usually help you understand not only what they say, but also what they mean.
3. Focus your whole attention on what they are saying, making mental notes on how what they say will affect you.
4. Do not decide how you will answer someone before they finish telling you what they want you to hear.
5. Repeat back to the speaker what you heard them say in your own words, so they can confirm or correct that what you heard was what they meant.
6. When you have time, during or after the conversation, write down what the speaker said, and what actions they want you to take. Written notes will help you remember what they said and what you are to do.
7. If, at the time you are to take the specified action, you are uncertain about the facts, confirm with the speaker what you plan to do, and ask if that is what they want.

There are also some guidelines for speakers:

1. Define what you want the listener to "take away" from your talk, and prepare your talk around those take aways.
2. Make eye contact with the listener.
3. Present your talk in a measured pace.
4. Emphasize key points with inflections in your voice.
5. Be aware of your nonverbal cues for what message they are transmitting.

Since most people do not use active listening, they may have disadvantages in their careers. They misunderstand what is expected, do the task incorrectly, or do something their manger did not ask for. By learning and using active listening practices, you can boost your career by ensuring that you are receiving your manager's communications correctly.

Give Generously
It is more blessed to give than to receive.

When we are born, we are 100 percent self-centered. The only concern of a baby is to get whatever they want NOW. As we grow up, we learn we have to give something to get what we want. We learn to smile and play happy, and when our parents see that, they think we are doing it for them, so we get what we want. This give-and-take continues throughout our lives. When we get a gift from Grandma, we scream with delight, even if we don't like the gift, so Grandma will keep buying us gifts for the rest of our lives.

The challenge many have as they mature is that they remain in this give-and-take mindset—believing that all giving must be reciprocated in quid pro quo fashion. Too many people believe that what they have is totally theirs, and no one besides them has any right to their money. They operate as if the goal of life is in hoarding as many resources as possible.

The lesson many forget is that the joy of receiving is often exceeded by the joy of giving.

A major principle about how the world works is give-and-take. If you want to earn money, you have to trade your time and talents for a paycheck. If you want to buy a dress, you have to pay cash for it. If you want someone to do a favor for you, you have to be willing to do a favor for them.

For many transactions, the price is defined; however, for some items, such as a car, if the price listed is more than you want to pay, you can try to negotiate a better price. For some products and services, the price is optional, but the person serving you may suggest a price, such as when a software developer offers an app that is free to download but requests a donation to cover costs. For other purchases, you can enjoy what they're offering, and afterward determine how much you will give for the performance; this pricing model is sometimes used in small theater and music venues. Some people feel that when someone is paid to do a job, you do not need to pay them any extra, such as restaurant servers or valet parking drivers. However, rather than give nothing, you give the smallest amount you think will be sufficient.

There are two types of generosity: one is giving of self, the other is giving resources.

Giving of self includes actions you take, such as thanking people for what they have done, serving on a committee for a charity, or making time in your schedule to teach a colleague a new skill.

Giving of resources may include money, stocks, possessions, or property. These are resources you could use for yourself, but instead you give to others for their benefit.

Many people follow a well-accepted money management principle, which is to give 10 percent of your take-home pay to charity, put 10 percent in savings, and live on the remaining 80 percent. Similarly, a rule of thumb for evaluating charities is to only donate to charities that spend 15 percent of their income or less on fundraising.

What type of people give to charities, and how much do they give? Most charities receive 80 percent of their income from 20 percent of their supporters; this includes churches. The Bible recommends that Christians give 10 percent (a tithe) of their income to their church. A low percentage actually do. Churches find that the rich give 2 percent of their income, and poor people give 3 percent.

The Giving Pledge is a movement that, according to its website, encourages "billionaires, or those who would be if not for their giving, to publicly commit to give the majority of their wealth to philanthropy either during their lifetimes or in their wills." Bill Gates, founder of Microsoft, and Warren Buffett, CEO of Berkshire Hathaway, are the founders of this movement.

Gates told his children that he would pay for their education but provide them with no more money for the rest of his life. Buffet did something similar. They know how much trouble kids get into when they have too much money.

Why do the people who give away 10 percent or more of their income do it? One of the major reasons is that they feel they have been blessed with wealth in life, and they want to pay it forward to others. Many people of faith believe that we are blessed to be a blessing to others. This principle is found in the story of Abraham, to whom God says, "I will bless you; I will make your name great, and you will be a blessing" (Genesis 12:2–3, NIV). Many give their Christian church 10 percent of their income simply because the Bible says they should. Some people give because they want to say thanks for what has happened to them or family member. For example, they or a family member were healed from cancer, so they donate to support cancer research. Or they received a scholarship to school that enabled them to be successful, so they repay the organization by funding scholarships for future students. Others believe in a cause, for example, helping the homeless, and donate to help advance that cause.

Why should I give my time or money away? There are many reasons:

  • To support a cause or religious group you believe in.

- To promote the work of a charity you have established.
- To advance the work of an organization that will take action you want to see happen.
- To help individuals or organizations you care about, such as veterans, homeless people, or a college.
- To provide small gifts to many organizations you feel are doing the right thing.

If I give substantial amounts of time and money away, will I be rewarded? Yes, but you should not give time and money away to be rewarded. Generosity should come from your heart; it should always be something you want to do, not something you are obligated to do.

As Jesus said, "It is more blessed to give than to receive" (Acts 20:35, NIV), and also "Give, and it will be given to you . . . For with the measure you use, it will be measured to you" (Luke 6:38, NIV). A pastor once told me you cannot out-give God—the more you give, the more you will get.

My plan was to make a living and enjoy my work—not to become rich. We had no goals; we just thanked God for whatever income we received. When we earned more income than we needed for our standard of living, we gave it away. When we did, our income increased. When our income increased, so did our giving, and again we got more income, and the cycle repeated. Are we unique? No. We have heard or read about hundreds of people with the same story.

Whether it's with your time, your talent, or your treasure, you can either be self-centered or generous. Try being generous. It works.

Use Your Free Will for Good
Having a free will means you can use it
to do whatever you want—don't fall into the trap
of using it for self-centered means.

God gave every person a free will to be able to do what they want. God also wants every person to be prosperous—to that end he gave us a money management plan on how to use our wealth. Likewise, he has given each of us a plan for managing the use of our free will. This is a two-part plan:

Part One—When we are baptized, we received, as a free gift from God, the Holy Spirit, which helps us know right from wrong and is a means for God to communicate with us.

Part Two—God gave us a brain to chart a path for our lives, and to think about how we will live our lives. As one thinks, so one is (Proverbs 23:7, paraphrased), meaning we become who we think we are. Let us try to explain how our attitude about life comes from who we think we are. Visualize your brain divided into two parts—the world's part and God's part. The world's part is divided into hate, fear, anger, and doubt. If you use your free will to focus on the world's part, you can become cynical, hate your neighbor, and feel cheated by the world for not giving you enough respect and rewards. If you use your free will to use your brain to follow God's way, that part is divided into love, joy, peace, and hope. If you focus on God's way, you will worship God with all your heart, soul, and mind; love your neighbor; be content and joyful; love life; be generous; and believe your hopes for the future will come true.

For parents, grandparents, and others with influence on children, one of the best things we can do is to help them use their free will to follow God's plan to achieve their destinies.

You are a beloved child of God, and he wants you to use your brain to achieve the destiny he wants for you. The world's way makes it almost impossible to achieve God's destiny for you.

I believe God has made it easy for you to use your free will to follow his will for you. However, you must want to follow God's will to make it happen. You must be baptized; listen to what the Holy Spirit tells you to do; and focus your brain on love, joy, peace, and hope. It is a choice you can make using your free will.

How do you do that? First: stop worrying; don't let fear stop you from doing what is right, don't be angry at people, and start believing your future will be wonderful. Second: be thankful to God, and have regular prayer sessions with God to allow him to guide your life by telling you what to do—but when he tells you, you must do it yourself, with his help.

Accentuate the Positive and Eliminate the Negative
You are born with skills and talents—build on them.

When I was in elementary school, my music teacher told me to mouth the words of a song instead of trying to sing them. Everyone can do some things well, and other things poorly. Why then do parents, teachers, guidance counselors, and performance appraisers focus on improving what you do poorly? Because they don't understand that the time you spend trying to improve your weaknesses would be better spent improving your strengths. I was good at math, poor at singing. It would have been a waste of time to enroll me in a music school. It appears what employers are trying to do is make you mediocre at everything instead of making you an expert at what you do well. It makes no sense. The song "Accentuate the Positive, Eliminate the Negative" tells it all.

Evaluating your performance and building your career is too important to leave to your boss. By the time you graduate from high school, you should know what you are good at and what you cannot do well. If you're not sure, try a skills-based task and evaluate that skill. Businesses will reward you well for what you do well, but will not reward you on what you don't do well. Tell potential employers what you can do well, and be honest about your weakness so you don't fall into a job you are not qualified for. Sing the song "I Want to Be Me" and sell that "me" to future employers.

Beware of performance appraisals. It is highly likely the person giving you the appraisal is not trained in how to do it, and they probably don't know exactly what you do. You must realize you do three jobs at work: the job in your job description, the job you actually do, and the job you're appraised on. You may never know which of those you're being appraised on. The appraiser works off of a checklist that's usually designed to evaluate a mediocre employee. If the appraiser marks you low in an area, they will advise you on how you can develop that skill.

Dr. W. Edwards Deming believed the performance appraisal practice is the worst practice used in business because it is only done once a year and doesn't give an accurate assessment of what you do. Dr. Deming said you should be evaluated every day on what you do, so that if you need improvement you can work on it now, not a year from now.

In his article "The New Rules of Success in a Post-Career World," published by *The Wall Street Journal* on June 3, 2023, Bruce Feiler cited a 2018 study by Shawn Achor and colleagues that found "nine out of ten workers were willing to give up a quarter of their entire life earnings in exchange for work that's meaningful."

Feiler identified three conditions that make a person successful in their work.

First is **finding a job you're happy doing**. Feiler does not specifically mention skills, but that is implied. He wrote, "Much of our discourse about work focuses primarily on how to get a job. The problem with this approach is that it usually works: You find a job, you maintain the appearance of success. But you won't necessarily be fulfilled, because you won't have taken the time to identify what actually makes you happy, and soon enough you'll be back where you started," which is to say, looking for a new job. So the first condition is finding a job that will make you happy, which means you will have to identify what makes you happy before you look for a job.

The second condition is **believing that the work you do is meaningful**. In other words, you will help others as well as doing job tasks. Studies like Feiler's show that millions of Americans still view money and wealth as very important. However, a growing segment of workers believe that having meaningful work is more important than money. Feiler cites a 2017 paper by researchers Jing Hu and Jacob Hirsch, who found, "If workers consider a job meaningful, they're willing to accept salaries that are 32 percent lower than for work that isn't." Ben Conniff, who stepped back from his position as co-founder of an $80 million a year seafood company to focus on sustainability initiatives, told Feiler, "There's a role in business for people like me. People who put purpose over profit...people will realize that there's value in values."

The third condition is, in Feiler's words, "Success is a story, not a status":

> The final new rule of success may be the most consequential: Success is not fixed; it's ever-changing. It's not a destination; it's a narrative. Freed from the myth of the corporate ladder and confronting multiple opportunities to rethink our work stories, many of us are making choices that serve our varied needs at different times in our lives.

> When there is no single definition of success, there is no penalty for choosing your own definition.

Feiler goes into more depth on this topic in his book *The Search: Finding Meaningful Work In a Post-Career World*.

When fulfilled, these three conditions allow you to accentuate the positive and eliminate the negative. You must find what success is by using your own standard, for example, where you want to live, the type of work that makes you happy, and the level of income that is enough for your needs. You decide the value of the work you do, not your boss using a corporate appraisal checklist.

CHAPTER ELEVEN

MMTs for Growing Your Career

Your improvement and advancement are
too important to leave to anyone else.

BECOMING MORE SUCCESSFUL AND being better rewarded should be top priorities for everyone in business. Most bosses think about their careers first and those of others second. You may be able to get help from your boss, but do not rely on them completely. You must accept the responsibility of advancing your own career, because when your career conflicts with your boss's, you may lose.

Early in this book ("Modern Miracles"), I told the story of how I secured a $500,000 grant from IBM for the nonprofit I worked for. The project was very successful, and everyone was pleased—except the president of my association, who thought that I, as a lowly project manager, got more credit than he did. So I was fired.

Ross Perot, perhaps IBM's best salesman ever, one year reached the maximum bonus he could receive, so he wouldn't get another bonus until the following year. He quit IBM and started his own company, Electronic Data Systems, which was very successful.

These examples show that when a subordinate outshines the boss, they are sometimes seen as threats. That's why you cannot rely on your boss to advance your career.

Other challenges in many organizations can inhibit career growth. These include pay grade limitations; inadequate training or mentoring by managers; and the inability to advance unless someone above you retires, gets promoted, or quits. Managers' favorites get promoted and receive better mentoring and larger pay raises than others who deserve it. Coworkers who think they deserve what you have earned can also make life miserable for everyone.

Managing your own career is a skill most people do not have—but you can learn it. The following MMTs can help you manage your own career.

Do the Donkey Duties
If you are willing to do what others will not,
your job is more secure.

Donkeys can carry 20 percent to 30 percent of their body weight on their backs, and on level ground can pull up to twice their body weight. For these reasons and others, donkeys have been used as pack animals since ancient times, and *donkeywork* is a synonym for tedious or labor-intensive work.

Many workers today, feeling overworked and underpaid, will do the bare minimum specified in their job description. If you are willing to do a little donkeywork, you can set yourself apart from those workers.

When my son took a job at Lockheed Martin, a contractor told him to seek jobs no one else wanted to do. The reason? As a defense and aerospace company, Lockheed Martin lives off government contracts. When a contract ends, there is no longer a need for the people working on that project. Layoffs generally follow. For example, the end of the US Space Shuttle program in 2011 led to 8,000 people being laid off in Florida ("End Of Shuttle Program Leaves Thousands Jobless," NPR, July 7, 2011).

However, a company may retain highly skilled and dedicated workers by transferring them to other projects that are still active. My son took the contractor's advice and has lasted through multiple layoffs over twenty-five years.

Doing tasks no one wants to do need not—in fact, should not—be your full-time job. But you can make time in your day to make copies, package boxes, organize an unkempt supply room, or arrange an office party.

Volunteering for tasks that are outside your normal scope of work demonstrates to managers that you have ambitions beyond your job description. As Rick Whitted writes in his book *Outgrowing Your Space at Work*, "You don't get promoted . . . You outgrow the space you're in. When that happens, a bigger space will be made for you."

Along with improving your competencies, doing the donkeywork helps you outgrow your current position. Building a reputation for doing whatever needs to be done shows management that you will do anything that's necessary for the success of your team.

Recently there have been several articles about entrepreneurs looking for jobs no one wants to do, and making a good living from doing those jobs. Two that are often cited are, first, cleaners who scour residents' trash cans after the garbage is collected; and second, cleaning up messes left by pets in dog owners' backyards. As I walk my neighborhood, I see a van providing mobile dog grooming services, and a truck whose driver washes and polishes clients' cars. People are willing to pay others to do the jobs they don't want to do. Which is to say there is value in doing the donkeywork.

Many of those doing jobs no one wants to do get little recognition. I have to walk every day for rehabilitation, so I decided that during my walks I would pick up trash. Few ever comment on what I do.

There is a famous passage in the Bible about Jesus riding a donkey into Bethlehem. Where does the donkey come from? All we know is that two unnamed disciples go pick up the donkey from its unnamed owner. Although a donkey carrying an adult man is surely doing donkey's work, one could also say that the person taking care of the donkey is doing, as I like to call it, donkey duties. It's a good term for doing what others don't want to do.

Why would anyone want to do donkey duties? There are many reasons. I pick up trash because I want to live in a clean neighborhood. When we opened our business, we like many small business owners did whatever was necessary, including donkeywork, to be successful. When the boss or owner pitches in on the donkey duties, the workers also feel inspired to do those tasks. Some people are helpful by nature, so when they see a fellow worker overloaded at work, they lend a hand.

Why should you do donkey duties when no one wants to? Because it is the right thing to do. Don't think in the moment about being recognized or rewarded. Those things may come later in a form that surprises you.

You Gotta Have Hope
"If you can dream it, you can do it."—Walt Disney

Without hope, nothing will ever change, because if you don't dream for, and work for, a better world, your world will never change. For example, if you hate your job, but don't believe you can get a better job, you won't.

People without hope are not only unhappy; they can get depressed to the point of either contemplating or even committing suicide. Hope is one part of a three-part process. The other two parts are faith and love.

Hope is the feeling that what you desire is likely to happen.

Faith is trust in something that can fulfill your hopes.

Love is the action you take to express your faith.

I like to think of these three parts this way: hope is the work of your heart, faith is the work of your mind, and love is the work of your hands.

Without hope, you will not believe things can be changed; without faith, you will not know how to make life better; and without love, what you hope for will never happen.

For example, you have hope that a promotion will provide the right job, you have faith that your skills can earn you that promotion, and your love inspires you to do the hard work needed to earn that promotion.

If you think love is a feeling, you need to expand your view. As the saying goes, love is a verb. One way we love others is by serving them, such as when we bring a meal to a sick friend.

The Bible says that with God nothing is impossible (Luke 1:37), so if you believe in God, that is all the hope you need.

According to MarketWatch, about 20 percent to 50 percent of workers would leave their jobs if they won the lottery ("Would you quit your job if you won the lottery? Many say no," May 27, 2016). But this is very dependent on the type of job. People in low-paying and unsatisfying jobs were more likely to quit.

My experience shows that it is the benefits that keep many people from leaving their jobs. Benefits are called the golden handcuffs because they keep you from quitting your job. I've known many employees around age fifty-five that start counting the number of months they have to work until they can retire, and plan to say in their current job until retirement sets them free.

Both of these conditions reveal a lack of hope. Why don't more people have hope? Every person's reason is probably unique: their parents told them they were no good; they failed in school or in their job; they lack confidence; or they have accepted that others will tell them what to do, so they don't have to think.

This is why I wanted my grandchildren to go to a church school. The school I wanted required each teacher to tell each child something they did good every day. From their first year in school they had to perform something in front of the class, at least once a week, and they had to participate in sports or artistic events to learn how to work with a team. They learned about God and were taught that how you play a game is more important than winning. By the time they graduated, they were ready to take on the world and win.

If you haven't been adequately prepared to face the world, what can you do? Two things.

First, be happy. You can control whether or not you want to be happy. You can be happy going to an event like a Taylor Swift concert or a sporting event, but even a good joke can lift your spirits.

Other ways to foster your own happiness include eating healthfully, engaging in physical activity you enjoy, planning to do something fun after work that you can look forward to all day, doing your job well even if no one else cares, bringing small candies to work to give yourself a treat every hour, and thinking about happy experiences you have had in the past.

Increase your pride by improving your skills, for example by taking a public speaking course, learning a new computer skill, or taking an online course.

You may be surprised when people ask you why you are happy, tell them "I love my life," and believe it.

If something bad happens, shake it off. This is easier said than done, and it does require acknowledging the harm. In his article "Faith, hope(lessness), and recovery," Dr. Glenn Doyle writes, "Let that hopeless, hurt part of you exist. Don't demand it shut up, don't demand it go away. Let it say its piece. It's a part of you, and its voice is valid. It has a right to be heard. But it doesn't have a right to derail you."

Shaking off hopelessness, whether it comes from your own failure or someone else's action against you, requires acknowledging the harm while still having faith in your skills to overcome the setback.

Second, know what you want to be. If you do not know where you are going, all roads lead there. You must decide what to hope *for*. Pretend you are a guidance counselor, and as such ask yourself *what is the most important thing that could happen to you that would improve your life?*

Now you have something to hope for.

Next, ask yourself if you believe you alone could make that happen. Working with God, could you make it happen? If the answer is yes, hope for what you want, then figure out how you are going to make it happen.

Never give up on making it happen.

The Honesty Policy
Tell the truth, and it will set you free.

When confronted with a question about facts that you're uncomfortable answering, do you lie or tell the truth? There are consequences either way. If you tell the truth, you may be punished. If you lie and are caught lying, you may be punished.

If you've done wrong and lied about it, you will not only be guilty of the wrongdoing, but also guilty of lying. Normally when one is guilty on two counts, the punishment is be greater than for the one wrongdoing.

When I was a teenager, I had a summer job in the kitchen of a restaurant. The job promised a twelve-week bonus if I stayed on through Labor Day.

While fooling around on a slow day, I broke a kitchen instrument that was used frequently. Nobody saw what I did, so I put the broken instrument in the outside trash.

When my supervisor asked if I knew what happened to it, I lied to avoid punishment.

After a short investigation, during which the broken instrument was found, I confessed. I was allowed to work until Labor Day, but forfeited the bonus.

My lesson about lying was never forgotten, and after that I always prided myself on telling the truth.

Why is telling the truth considered a Managing Management Tactic? Because too many people either lie or shift the blame onto someone else.

How can telling the truth set you free? When you lie, you know you are lying and have to live with that. You must keep reinforcing the false information to others when you know it's untrue. Everybody has a conscience that keeps telling them they have done something wrong. Some people lose sleep over it. Once you confess your guilt and accept responsibility for your deed, you no longer have to hide your lies.

When you accept responsibility, you should be ready to accept punishment.

In the early days of one huge corporation, a senior vice president bungled a major, million-dollar project. At the end of a year, the project was a dismal failure and cancelled. The CEO called the vice president into his office, asking for an explanation regarding the failure.

The vice president confessed that the failure was due to his bad decisions and poor management. He told the CEO he expected to be fired.

The CEO told the vice president, "I cannot fire you. I have just spent a million dollars teaching you how not to manage a project."

Execution of this tactic is simple: when you are asked a question, answer truthfully. Tell the truth, the whole truth, and nothing but the truth. Accept responsibility for your actions and expect punishment if you deserve it.

Even better, if you know the truth *before* your misdeed is discovered, tell the person or persons involved what you did so they can take any action needed to correct your misdeed. Lastly, work to resolve the situation to the best of your ability.

The Blue Mold Tactic
Like cheese, until a person has a coating of mold,
they are not considered valuable.

Blue mold is a variety of fungus that produces bluish spores that are used to ripen cheeses and which give those cheese a unique color and texture. Blue cheese is valued by the amount of mold in it.

The same concept can be used to explain the role of experience in organizations. Consider blue mold analogous to years of experience. The greater your number of years of experience, the more valuable you are to your organization. People respect experience, and will reward this blue mold by awarding larger salaries based on years of experience.

However, there comes a point when cheese get too moldy and starts to lose value. When the mold loses value, organizations talk about bringing in "new blood" (a different type of cheese) to infuse the organization with new life.

One Christmas evening, we could not get a string of tree lights to work. Our older son was a college graduate in engineering; he got out his electrical equipment and began searching for the problem.

No luck; he gave up.

Our younger son, who tinkered with electrical circuits, found the problem in three minutes.

Which is better, education or experience?

Mold grows slowly. So does experience. My older son was accepted for a job at Lockheed Martin as an engineer working on government contracts. When a contact ended, so did many jobs. Employees with experience related to the contract were only valuable to that particular contract.

A friend told him to work on the old equipment because nobody wanted to. So when problems occurred with that old equipment, my son was the only one who could fix it. That experience—his blue mold—meant he was less likely to be laid off.

In today's highly technical world, mold is still king, until how the work is done changes.

The presence or absence of mold determines how employees are viewed in most organizations. Often, employees are judged not by what they can do, but by the amount of blue mold they have accumulated. Another definition of *blue* is that it's how many employees feel as they wait long enough for enough blue mold to grow on them so they can get more responsibility.

An interesting fact about mold is that the higher the rate of turnover in your department, the faster your mold grows. When management is faced with a personnel decision, they often take the easy way out. What is that? They choose the employees with the most mold.

The Blue Mold Tactic applies in a number of ways. For instance, when an IT manager has to decide which computers to buy, they usually make a safe choice, which is that they choose the same equipment as most experienced IT managers.

Years ago, I was on a committee to decide which computers should be acquired to replace our computers. At that time, there were only eight computer companies—we called them IBM and the seven dwarfs. Although one company's computers were far from the best, that company provided the best service.

A computer department manager would know that if they bought those computers and things went wrong, they would not be blamed, because senior executive, and most experienced computer department managers, liked the company. As far as most executives are concerned, blue chip and blue mold are the same thing.

But if the manager bought from one of the dwarfs and the computers failed to perform, the manager would be blamed because they didn't pick what the executives thought best.

My committee picked that company.

Management's viewpoint toward blue mold equipment and personnel lead to the following conclusions:

- Your probability of winning an argument is proportional to your mold thickness. In other words, if you are short on mold, you are likely to lose.
- If you are uncertain as to which product or person is best for the job, make your choice based on mold thickness. If the project fails, management will consider you have been given an impossible task.
- If you don't believe in the Blue Mold Tactic, be prepared to work like hell to make the project successful. If you don't consider blue mold in your decision, blue mold will come back to haunt you.

How do you make the Blue Mold Tactic work for you?

1. If you depend on your blue mold to ensure your continuous employment, beware of workers younger than you. Younger workers often believe they know everything, and do not want to do things the way they have always been done. In their opinion, blue mold veterans are obsolete. Focus your career on your ability to identify and solve problems using your experience. Take time to explain to younger workers *why* things are done a certain way, remembering that *because we've always done it that way* is an insufficient answer.

2. If your management, especially your boss, employs Blue Mold Tactics, you are okay. Preach that that although newer workers may make mistakes, the blue mold veterans can discover and correct those mistakes before they become too costly, and can train the newer workers to prevent errors in the future.

The Potted Plant Theory
There is more to life than money and power.

How do you know if you have made it? The vice president knows her niche in the hierarchy when she pulls into the underground parking lot and parks in her reserved spot next to the elevator. The corporate controller knows it when he walks into his office on the top floor of the building. The administrative assistant knows it when the pick up their white telephone with three incoming lines. And, I must admit, my ambition in the company was to have my own office complete with a potted plant watered by the company gardener.

Every organization has its own status symbols.

In one large insurance company, a person's status can be determined by the number of ceiling tiles in their office.

At Kodak, when an employee reached their twenty-fifty anniversary with the company, they got a George Eastman Trophy, which all displayed on their desks, to the envy of those who hadn't gotten one yet.

To many people, status symbols are more important than money. The higher you go, the snazzier the rewards. Remember how you used to judge people's wealth when you were a kid? The kid whose mother bought her kid an ice cream bar every day was just a notch above everyone else's mother. The first kid on the block to get a bike was looked up to buy one and all. Ten-speed bikes were better than five-speed bikes. The ones who bought their lunch at school were better than those who brown bagged it. And so on...

When we grew up and moved into the business world, we found things haven't changed much. High-status workers have parking spaces near the elevator. Important people have offices with views. And yes, even less important people like me have potted plants in their offices. Low-status workers don't have any of these things.

There was once a survey conducted in New York City during the fall, which asked people on the street to observe those coming up from the subway and identify which people were executives, and which were not? Many people said the workers with light-colored overcoats were executives, because they could afford to have their coats cleaned, and those with dark overcoats were workers who could not pay for cleaning. Similarly, as a woman with a briefcase and a man without one left a building to get a cab, bystanders were asked which was the boss, and all said the person with the briefcase must be the boss.

In the cold cruel world of business, you can tell "high-status" people from "low-status" people by the status symbols they own. There are two rules you must honor regarding status symbols:

1. If you are given a status symbol, don't reject it. Give great thanks for it, even though you may think it is simple or silly.
2. Anyone owning a status symbol should be honored to have it. Making fun of the person who displays it in their office is making fun of your management, which is not a good tactic for getting ahead.

Status symbols may strike you as frivolous or funny. But the truth is, they can be worth more than money as indicators of your position in the workplace hierarchy.

Spinning Plates Theory
You can only keep so many plates spinning before one breaks, but management doesn't know this.

If you're old enough, you will have seen an old vaudeville act in which a performer kept a large number plates spinning high in the air on thin sticks. It looked as though there might be no limit to the number of plates, but the performer knew his limit and worked accordingly.

Every day in the business world, workers are forced to perform the spinning plates act. The difference is that the manager refuses to admit that workers can only spin a limited number of plates. So the managers keep stacking them up on their performers. If the manager sees that Will Workman has six plates spinning, and they are all spinning well, he will add a seventh plate and then an eighth, and so on until Will shouts "no more plates" or one falls to the ground and shatters. If one falls, the manager assumes that Will is incompetent and puts that plate on someone else's stack.

Plates in business take various forms: units sold, dollar volume, unit of work, projects, and so forth. For example, if you sell 100 cars this year, you may be asked to sell 110 next year and so on—eventually you will miss the quota and the plate will come crashing down.

At times, managers go crazy and throw a whole stack of plates on the pile. This might increase a salesperson's quota from 100 to 140 cars in just one year. In the business world, this is referred to as dumping on employees. If you were in production your next plate could be five units per day of increased production added to the plates you already have a spinning. If you accept the plate, you had better get it spinning and keep it spinning or you'll be labeled incompetent.

Whatever your job metric, it will be gradually increased until management finds your breaking point. As a worker, you must realize what is happening and be prepared to yell "no more plates" in a way that will convince but not alienate management. Not the least important is your timing.

How can you tell your boss "no more plates" without getting clobbered? One thing you must do is let a plate or two start falling toward the floor, and then, just before they crash, you get them going again. For example, if it appears that one of your projects will not be finished on time, you inform the boss and ask for a few more people to work the weekend to meet the deadline. As your boss watches you save the day time after time, he may conclude that you have all the plates you can handle.

There are several tactics in this book that may help convince your boss to stop dumping more plates on your desk:

Trial Balloon—send up the idea of giving the new plate to someone else or the idea of giving an already spinning plate to another worker when you accept a new plate. Another trial balloon might be the statement, "I don't know if I can keep any more plates spinning." If your boss seems agreeable to these or other trial balloons, make a concrete suggestion.

Man on the Moon—This requires you to accept any number of plates, but request plenty of help in spinning them.

Alibi File—since you know sooner or later a plate will fall, build a complete file ahead of time so you can place blame appropriately.

Rathole Theory—swipe the broken pieces down the rathole and ask for a new plate.

If spinning plates have you berserk, pick a theory and go to work.

Waiting Time Is Not Wasted Time
Few people have more than a handful of opportunities during their lifetimes, so use waiting time to prepare yourself for such chances when they arise.

In life there is a time for everything: a time to learn, a time to play, a time to work, a time to serve others, and a time to accept the opportunity offered to you.

If you don't know what your next opportunity is going be, how can you prepare yourself for it? At any age, you know what you like and what you don't like, what you can do well and what you do poorly, who you are and what you want to become. Add to this knowledge your life experiences, and you have a base from which you can prepare for what you want to be. You can deduce what other things you should learn and do to prepare you for accepting opportunities when they arise.

Once an eagle hatches from its shell, far above the ground, it begins preparing for flight. The baby watches his mother fly, and knows that is what he wants to do. After his mother knows he is strong enough to fly, he must decide to jump out of the nest, performing a do or die flight. If he is afraid to jump, his mother will push him out of the nest. As the eagle flies, he must learn to use his wings to soar. This skill requires him to lock his wings outward so he can soar for long periods of time looking for prey.

What does this story say about preparing yourself for opportunities? Like the eagle's mother, your family, teachers, coaches, guidance counselors, and pastors will help motivate you and develop the skills you need. If you want to be a musician, you must learn the scales and the basics of music to get into a band or orchestra. It took me until I was forty-two years old to get enough knowledge and experience to start a quality assurance trade association. During that time, I had to do many things I preferred not to do, waiting until I felt I was prepared to start my own business.

Waiting and preparing for something is a biblical concept thousands of years old. It is best expressed in Isaiah 40:31 which states, "But they that wait upon the LORD shall renew their strength; they shall mount up with wings as eagles; they shall run, and not be weary; and they shall walk, and not faint." (For the word LORD, you may substitute whatever suits your faith tradition.)

What we believe this is saying is that if you wait for the right time to achieve your destiny (or goal), during that time you will have the strength to do those things needed for you to achieve your destiny. When the waiting period is over and you accept the opportunity that is presented to you, like the eagle you're pushed out of the nest—that is your waiting period is over. You will soar like an eagle as you are accepting the opportunity and working to be successful at it, because your preparation will have given you the skills and strength to succeed.

Waiting time is essential to becoming successful. When my wife and I started our business, we had to work long hours and travel extensively putting on programs just to keep our heads out of water. We had strong enough motivation to provide a positive start to our business.

Many businesses fail because they are not adequately prepared. In November 2022, tech entrepreneur Noam Bardin launched Post News, a social media site focused on journalism. Bardin had previously been CEO of Waze, a company that produced a successful navigation app. But in the spring of 2024, Bardin announced that Post News would be shutting down. The company had raised investor capital, but it seems that, without sufficient experience in social media or journalism, the leadership team was ill-prepared to grow the site's user base at a rate that would satisfy the investors.

Before accepting any opportunity, take all the time necessary to prepare for success. You're much better off turning down an opportunity rather than accepting it and failing. You also need to distinguish between good and bad opportunities. A good opportunity is one at which you know you can succeed because you are adequately prepared.

Grab The Brass Ring
If you see the brass ring waiting for you
to catch it—grab hold.

When I was a boy, I loved to ride the merry-go-round. An arm dispensing rings hung within reach of those riding an outside horse. Occasionally a brass ring was inserted among the steel rings, and if you caught it you could redeem it for a free ride. Unfortunately, some were either afraid to reach out to catch the ring, or they were distracted and the ring passed by them and into another person's hand. The same type of opportunities can occur in real life.

In the early days of computing, my boss Earl could perform magic with a computer. He talked about, and was encouraged to do so by his staff, starting a computer consulting group. It was a winning idea. However, he could not do it: the combination of feeling comfortable in his current job, the golden handcuffs (see Chapter

Seven), and the difficulty of building a business made it too hard for him to give up his job, so he stayed. At the same time, Ross Perot left IBM to start such a business, and it was an outstanding success.

If you are offered, or know about, a unique opportunity like Earl was, weigh it carefully. It may be the last opportunity you ever get in your life.

Many people ask, when a unique opportunity comes around, how can one know if it is the right opportunity for me? In my opinion, there are four conditions that, if met, will tell you an opportunity is right for you:

1. You know that if you take this opportunity, you will be successful.
2. It is a much better opportunity than you will get in your current position.
3. In your heart you know what you would be doing is exactly what you want to do
4. There is no deal-breaker you cannot resolve.

If an opportunity meets these four conditions, accept it. Note, there is no mention here of salary, position, power, or benefits. If you are not happy with your work, these features will not make you happy.

The statistics for accepting opportunities are bleak. The Gallup World Poll found that 85 percent of all workers do not like their jobs. In the USA, that number was 70 percent, but that is still a lot of people who feel stuck unless they win the lottery.

Most people over forty years of age don't believe they can get another job. Golden handcuffs work by making leaving an unsatisfying job too costly. When people reach a certain age—somewhere from their mid-thirties on—if they feel comfortable in their job, with okay pay and benefits, they can develop an unwillingness to take on the risk of looking for and accepting a better opportunity. At that point, they join the active retired and count the days until they qualify for real retirement. Of the small percent of workers that are left, most believe they have deal-beakers that prevents them from leaving their employer— for example, not being willing to move their family.

Opportunities can come to you in various ways:

1. You might hear of an opportunity by happenstance.
2. You may know that you have to move, so you must seek new employment in the new location.
3. You want a particular role in a new field, so you train and prepare for that job.
4. You actively search for an opportunity that will provide what you need in your career.
5. An opportunity is proactively offered to you because of your reputation.

As you can see, as your skills increase, so does your chances of being offered an opportunity.

When an opportunity arises, and you know you know it's a good one, what issues do you have to resolve before you can accept that opportunity?

1. Fear of the risks associated with the opportunity
2. The discomfort of giving up a job in which you are comfortable
3. Disruption of or opposition from your family
4. Golden handcuffs—the benefits you have now are less than the benefits associated with the opportunity
5. Salary reduction with the opportunity compared with what you now earn

How do you resolve these issues to allow you to take the opportunity? Let me explain how, using the five unique opportunities I had during my lifetime.

During college I met Cindy, whom I wanted to spend my life with. Marriage is a risk, but love resolved that for me.

During my first job in public accounting, I encountered a computer in 1960. I was amazed by what a computer could do, and immediately came to the conclusion that business in the future would revolve around computers. I looked for a leader in using computers and selected Kodak. I applied for and got a job as a programmer.

While at Kodak, I was transferred to the Internal Auditing Department against my wishes, but I learned so much in the early days of auditing computers, I become recognized as an innovator in that field.

I became aware of and applied for a job with the Institute of Internal Auditors and got it. It required moving to Florida (this was no issue) and taking a 30 percent cut in salary. This might have been an issue, but the salary offered was enough to allow us a decent living. More importantly, I was freed from a job, and boss, that I hated.

Our last unique opportunity came when I was fired for being too competent and well known, much more so than the president of the IIA. He wanted to be the top-dog, so I had to go. Cindy told me it was a sign from God to start our own business, which we did. Our only business then was to enjoy our jobs every day, and by doing that we were unbelievably successful.

Many people tell me that following their dream was the best thing they ever did, even if they weren't successful. If they had played it safe, they probably would have regretted not grasping the brass ring.

Using MMTs to Make Miracles

Business colleges do not teach MMTs
because there is no room in their curriculum
for innovative business practices.

WHEN I STARTED MY first real job in 1968 at Kodak, it was like joining a family. Rochester was a company town. My life and that of my family centered around Kodak. Any event in Rochester had a Kodak night. My wife built her social life around Kodak employees and facilities—for example, Kodak owned a bowling alley family members could use. They even held our mortgage.

At the time I joined, there was a play on Broadway called *How to Succeed in Business Without Really Trying.* In that show, the song "Company Way" in which the singer acknowledged that it was okay to follow the company ways of doing things.

The hero in the play advanced his career by doing things like learning where his boss's boss went to college, then wearing that person's college shirt and singing the school's alma mater when that boss was around.

Most of the high school and college graduates from Rochester wanted to get a job with Kodak and stay there for their lifetime. My coworkers were my friends, and my social life was with my coworkers families. I was very content just to work there for my first ten years, but then I noticed things began to change slowly, as the culture of our country changed.

When I was hired, I was twenty-seven years old, which was considered old to be hired by Kodak; they wanted to bring employees up in the Kodak way, and they believed the Kodak way was the best way. I was told if I did not like my role, they would find me another position at Kodak that I would like.

When employees are tied to their employer with golden handcuffs, they become apathetic and patiently wait for advancement. I felt a need to find ways around management and was not content to do things the company way.

That was how I started making the notes that eventually turned into this book. The original edition sold very well. In today's business environment, with strong generational differences, diversity in the workplace, and a polarized political environment, a new edition seemed necessary.

In the 1960s and 1970s, people's attitude toward work was that they needed work to live. There were few government safety nets. Liking one's job was not the most important thing in their lives. Culturally, employees sought out work that paid well enough, not on work that was meaningful enough.

That was then, and now is now. As noted earlier ("Accentuate the Positive"), Millennial and Gen Z workers seek meaningful work and place work/life balance as their top priority, far above salary. Bruce Feiler writes in his book *The Search: Finding Meaningful Work In a Post-Career World* that most of these workers are "motivated by events outside of the workplace. Something happens with our families, our health or our mindsets that causes us to rethink our employment."

These workers would be willing to take a 32 percent pay cut for a job with greater meaning. Similarly, when I left Kodak in 1974 to take a job making 27 percent less, that to me was the second best decision I ever made. Marrying my wife was number one.

How can MMTs help people find more meaningful work? These tactics help eliminate or minimize the impact of organizational roadblocks, micromanagement, and the impact of policies, rules, and regulations that stop workers from doing their work effectively and efficiently. These things take the fun out of work. MMTs alone will not make a worker happy, but they can eliminate those things that make them unhappy.

How do workers get motivated to use MMTs in their work, knowing that using them carries risks? It's a three step process:

1. Learn and master a new and effective skill set not taught in business schools.
2. Use your new skill set by doing only those things that are in the best interest of your employer. In other words, do the right thing for your employer when needed.
3. Accept the fact that the worst thing your employer can do to is fire you (or make your life so uncomfortable that you resign). If you have been doing the right thing for your employer, being fired or resigning may be the best thing that ever happened to you. I was fired three times and each time got a better job. Why? My confidence in myself had grown through the use of MMTs.

Workers like to use their brains and experience to make them more productive and proud of their contributions. Manage Management Tactics can help you do that and can advance your career by improving your skills, capabilities, and attitudes, as well as increasing your motivation to succeed. When you succeed, you will receive the recognition and rewards you deserve.

NOW THAT YOU HAVE READ THIS BOOK, IT'S TIME FOR YOU
TO START DOING WHAT IS RIGHT WITHOUT PERMISSION

⛰ THE END ⛰

www.ingramcontent.com/pod-product-compliance
Lightning Source LLC
Chambersburg PA
CBHW071552200326
41519CB00021BB/6719